Data Products Volume 1: From Projects to Products

Ownership, Governance, and Business Value

Amy Raygada

Technics Publications
SEDONA, ARIZONA

TECHNICS PUBLICATIONS

115 Linda Vista, Sedona, AZ 86336 USA

https://www.TechnicsPub.com

Edited by Steve Hoberman

Cover design by Lorena Molinari

First Printing 2026

Copyright © 2026 by Amy Raygada

ISBN, print ed.	9798898160616
ISBN, Kindle ed.	9798898160623
ISBN, PDF ed.	9798898160630

To the people who shaped this book without writing a word—
my son, my partner, my friends, my mentors, and the colleagues who
challenge and inspire me daily.

Endorsements

From projects to products, from tech-first to value-first. This book by Amy Raygada shows that data products succeed only when they are owned end-to-end, governed by design, and built around real human needs. Practical, honest, and refreshingly grounded in impact, this is a playbook for teams who want data products people actually use.

Winfried Adalbert Etzel
Data Governance Thinker, Writer, Host, Strategist, and Enthusiast

"Data Products Volume 1" is exactly the book the data community has been waiting for and Amy Raygada is exactly the person to write it. I am honored to call Amy a friend and a colleague, and I've seen firsthand how she lives what she writes about. This book doesn't just give you an overview of data products and their concepts - it gives you truly practical guidance on how to actually get started, including a 90 day roadmap that turns ideas into action. As the first part of a trilogy, it sets a great foundation for what's to come. This is a must-read for the thinkers AND the doers in the data community who want to stop talking about data products and start generating value with them. I'm so happy that others can now learn from Amy too!

Tiankai Feng
Author of "Humanizing Data Strategy" & "Humanizing AI Strategy"

All good things in the data space begin and end with customers. So too data products. Well done, Amy Raygada!

Tom Redman, The Data Doc

A compelling, insightful read offering fresh, structured perspectives on Data Products. Amy Raygada's engaging storytelling empowers leaders and practitioners with frameworks to identify high-impact opportunities, understand user needs, build strong business cases, and create lasting organizational success.

Tobias Rebele, Data & AI Platform Leader – DACH, Middle East & LATAM

Data governance ultimately depends on what you choose to govern. As data products increasingly become the primary governed entity, understanding what they actually are becomes critical. This book offers clarity. And by the end, you won't just own a Ferrari, but you'll understand how to make it drivable and people will want to get behind that wheel.

Säde Haveri, Data Management Professional and Entrepreneur

Based on concrete, real enterprise experience, Amy Raygada delivers a solid blueprint for building data products in the AI era.

Ole Olesen-Bagneux, Author, VP & Chief Evangelist, PhD

Amy Raygada delivers a practical, no-fluff guide that reframes "data work" into real products people actually adopt—grounded in user needs, clear ownership, and measurable business impact. Her frameworks make it easy to move from abstract strategy to day-to-day execution, without losing sight of governance, quality, and trust. The writing is sharp, relatable, and packed with lessons that will save teams from building "Ferraris nobody drives." If you're serious about turning data into outcomes—not just artifacts—Data Products, Volume 1 is the playbook you'll keep within arm's reach.

Jessica Talisman, Founder, Ontology Pipeline® and Contextually LLC

Amy didn't write a book — she built a flight manual for data. The Data Products Volume 1 is the most compact, actionable guide I've ever seen for navigating the real-life mess of data management work. Open any page, and you'll find complete clarity in under six sentences.

Aleksejs Plotnikovs, CDAO, Data Masterclass

Amy has a quite unique experience on Data & AI Products and impressively managed to condense it it this book... while keeping it really easy to read through. Full of very pragmatic tools, real stories and experiences, this first volume already covers a lot of key topics to approach Data Products in a holistic manner: processes, org models, roles, adoption & change, and of course how to assess value. The opening on AI Products, with their similarities and specificities, is brilliant!

Avoiding the typical traps of being too conceptual and buzzwordy, this is the perfect book for all Data & AI practitioners and leaders willing to put things in motion and build Data & AI products that actually have an impact. Can't wait for the next volumes!

Nicolas Averseng, Chief Product Officer, DataGalaxy

I highly recommend this book because it's written by someone who has been there and done it, blending real world experience with clear, actionable advice and guidance. What stood out most to me is how it goes beyond theory, using practical examples and case studies to show how data products actually work in real organisations. The concepts are easy to understand, yet deep enough to help modern data teams shift toward product thinking and focus on delivering measurable business value.

Darren Wood

Contents

Acknowledgments

This book exists because of the hundreds of data professionals, business leaders, and organizations I've had the privilege to work alongside through consulting engagements, conference presentations, and industry conversations. While client confidentiality prevents me from naming individuals, their collective wisdom and their willingness to share both spectacular successes and painful failures shaped every framework and recommendation you'll find here.

I'm especially grateful to the practitioners who shared their mistakes and failures. These honest reflections provided some of the most valuable insights in this book. It takes courage to admit when a million-dollar platform sits unused or when a "revolutionary" AI project never made it past the pilot phase.

The frameworks presented here have been battle-tested and refined through countless workshops, training sessions, and real-world implementations. Feedback from participants directly influenced not only the content but also how I've structured and presented every chapter.

Finally, this work stands on the shoulders of researchers, practitioners, and thought leaders who have advanced the fields of data management, product development, and organizational design. Their foundational contributions created the knowledge base that makes practical guides like this one possible.

Introduction

The Ferrari Nobody Drives

Let me start with a story that changed how I think about data forever. I was working with an e-commerce company that had built what they proudly called a "Ferrari of a data platform." It had all the latest technology, like streaming analytics, machine learning pipelines,[1] and beautiful architecture diagrams that belonged in a computer science textbook.

The platform cost them six figures to implement and took over 12 months to build. There was just one problem: nobody was using it. When I asked the business stakeholders why, their answers cut straight to the heart of our industry's biggest challenge:

- "We don't understand what's in there."
- "It's too complicated for our daily work."
- "We still get our reports from Excel because it's faster."
- "Nobody showed us how this helps us sell more or serve customers better."

The data team, meanwhile, was frustrated and demoralized. They had built exactly what they thought the business needed, using cutting-edge technology and following every best practice in the

---

[1] A pipeline is an automated workflow that moves data through a series of processing steps—from collection to transformation to delivery—without manual intervention.

book. Yet their masterpiece sat unused while business users continued their old workflows.

This disconnect between technical excellence and business adoption is why this book exists.

The Product Revolution That Data Missed

While data teams perfected their technical architectures, the rest of the business world underwent a product revolution. Companies learned to start with customer problems, not technical solutions. They discovered that adoption isn't an afterthought; it's a fundamental design requirement.

> The best technology in the world means nothing if humans can't or won't use it.

This product mindset transformed industries, but somehow data got left behind. We still celebrate technical achievements over business outcomes, measure success by pipeline elegance rather than decision enablement, and build what we think users should want instead of what they actually need.

> After more than a decade of watching organizations struggle with this disconnect, I've learned that the solution isn't better technology but instead better product thinking.

Why This Transformation Matters Now

This shift from projects to products fundamentally changes how we approach data work, and it's becoming critical for three key reasons:

- **Artificial intelligence is reshaping expectations.** AI systems demand new approaches to data quality and governance, where poor data quality can cause immediate, visible errors in customer-facing applications. New regulations, such as the EU AI Act, impose compliance requirements that directly affect how we build and manage data products.

- **Business users have evolved.** They've experienced well-designed consumer technology and expect the same from enterprise tools. They understand data's potential value but won't tolerate clunky interfaces or unclear business relevance.

- **The competitive landscape is accelerating.** Organizations that learn to turn data into business value quickly pull ahead. Those that struggle with adoption fall behind.

About the Series

The Data Product Management series provides a comprehensive roadmap for organizations transforming how they create, deliver, and sustain value from data. Rather than treating data product management as a single discipline, the series recognizes that success requires mastery across three interconnected domains: strategic intent, execution capabilities, and long-term sustainability.

Across the series, data governance serves as the umbrella concept for trust, quality, accountability, and compliance, while detailed data management practices are introduced progressively as implementation depth increases in later volumes. This structure reflects how organizations actually mature: starting with shared principles and operating models before diving into technical and operational mechanics.

This book establishes the foundational mindset shift from data-as-byproduct to data-as-product. It equips leaders and practitioners with frameworks for identifying high-value data product opportunities, understanding user needs, building compelling business cases, and creating the organizational conditions for success. Start here if you're asking "Why data products?" or "Where should we begin?"

Book 2 is about building data products, moving from strategy to execution by applying a technical guide covering architecture, design principles, platform engineering, and implementation. This book addresses functional and technical design, data product archetypes, platform capabilities, and the control plane infrastructure that enables self-service at scale. Turn here when you're ready to answer "How do we build this?"

Book 3 addresses what happens after launch: versioning, governance at scale, domain onboarding, team enablement, and lifecycle automation. This book ensures your data products deliver lasting value rather than becoming tomorrow's technical debt. This is your guide for "How do we make this work long-term?"

Who This Book Serves

This book is for anyone involved in turning data into business value:

- **Data and AI strategists** who need to build compelling business cases and drive organizational change. You'll find frameworks for communicating value, strategies for managing stakeholders, and roadmaps for scaling capabilities.

- **Product managers** transitioning into data product roles or working with data teams. You'll learn how product management principles apply to data, how to conduct user research in data contexts, and how to measure success.

- **Engineering leaders** who want to align technical excellence with business outcomes. You'll discover how to organize teams for product thinking, implement enabling governance, and build platforms that scale.

- **Business executives** who need to understand how to invest in and govern data initiatives. You'll get practical frameworks for evaluating investments, measuring ROI, and building data-driven cultures.

- **Consultants and advisors** helping organizations mature their data capabilities. You'll find assessment frameworks, transformation roadmaps, and change management strategies.

How This Book Is Organized

The book follows a logical progression from concepts to implementation:

- **Chapters 1-2** establish the foundation, including what data products are, why they matter, and how to organize teams for success.

- **Chapters 3-4** dive into operational aspects, including implementing enabling governance and measuring business value.

- **Chapters 5-6** focus on human and technical elements, including designing products people want to use and preparing for AI integration.

- **Chapter 7** provides immediate implementation guidance in the form of a practical 90-day action plan.

Each chapter includes frameworks you can apply immediately, real-world case studies, and reflection prompts tailored to your specific situation.

A Note on AI Integration

While this book comprehensively covers traditional data products, it also addresses emerging AI system requirements. The core principles remain the same, such as user focus, business value, and iterative improvement, but implementation details evolve.

You'll find specific guidance on AI governance, unstructured data management, and quality frameworks designed for machine learning systems.

The book treats AI not as a separate domain but as an evolution of data product thinking.

The Journey Ahead

This book isn't about perfect solutions or one-size-fits-all approaches. It's about practical frameworks I've seen work in the real world, honest conversations about what does and doesn't land, and strategies you can keep improving over time.

Before we talk about data products, we need to discuss foundations, because most failures don't come from a lack of talent or technology. They come from building fast without understanding where we're starting.

Chapter 1 picks up from that insight. It shows how to assess your current state honestly, understand your organizational blind spots, and see where product thinking actually fits. Before we can design the future, we have to know where we are today.

Let's begin that journey together.

ONE

Data Products Fundamentals

Beyond the Technical Excellence Trap

Before we dive into frameworks and methodologies, let's establish what we mean by "data as a product." This isn't buzzword engineering. Instead, it's a fundamental shift that determines whether your data initiatives create value or collect dust.

I learned this lesson working with a failed data platform. The platform was technically impressive with sophisticated analytics that could slice and dice data in dozens of ways. The problem? Field engineering managers, the intended primary users, logged in fewer than once per week.

When I interviewed them, I discovered the disconnect. The platform provided detailed analytics when they needed quick answers. It required training they didn't have time for. The data refreshed overnight when they needed real-time information during business hours. They had built a fancy platform when they needed simplicity and usability.

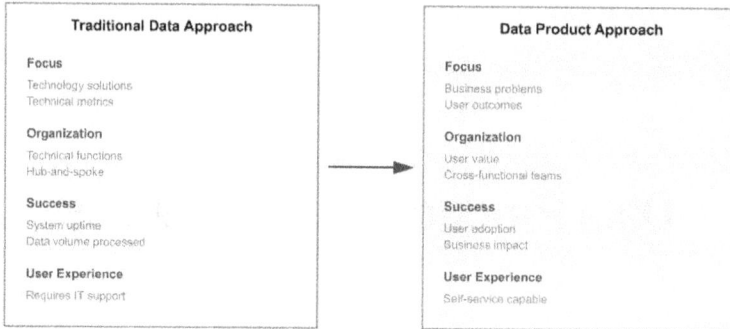

Traditional Data Approach	Data Product Approach
Focus	**Focus**
Technology solutions	Business problems
Technical metrics	User outcomes
Organization	**Organization**
Technical functions	User value
Hub-and-spoke	Cross-functional teams
Success	**Success**
System uptime	User adoption
Data volume processed	Business impact
User Experience	**User Experience**
Requires IT support	Self-service capable

Figure 1: Traditional versus Product Approach Comparison.

The traditional approach treats data as a byproduct of business operations. IT teams extract it, store it in warehouses, and create reports when asked.

The product approach treats data as something designed, developed, and managed like any other product your company creates, with clear users, value propositions, and success metrics.

This shift changes everything. Instead of asking "How can we build the best technical solution?" we ask "How can we solve real business problems for real users?"

Rather than organizing around technical functions, we organize around user value.

Defining Data Products Beyond the Buzzwords

A data product is not just a dataset sitting in a warehouse. It's a complete solution designed to solve business problems for specific users. True data products share five essential characteristics:

Five Essential Data Product Characteristics

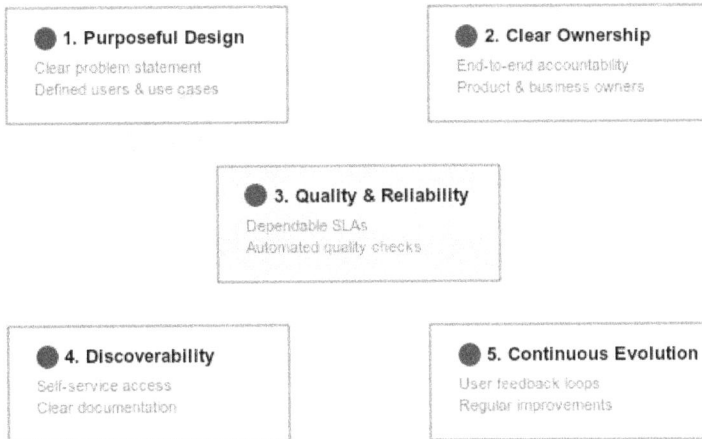

● 1. Purposeful Design
Clear problem statement
Defined users & use cases

● 2. Clear Ownership
End-to-end accountability
Product & business owners

● 3. Quality & Reliability
Dependable SLAs
Automated quality checks

● 4. Discoverability
Self-service access
Clear documentation

● 5. Continuous Evolution
User feedback loops
Regular improvements

Figure 2: Success requires excellence in all five characteristics.

- **Purposeful design** answers three fundamental questions: What specific business problem does this solve? Who are the primary users, and what job are they trying to get done? What actions will users take based on this data?

- **Clear ownership and accountability** include a technical owner who maintains pipelines and infrastructure, a business owner who understands the domain, and a data product manager who bridges technical and business concerns.

- **Quality and reliability standards** mean defined SLAs for freshness and availability, automated quality checks and monitoring, and clear error handling and user communication.

- **Discoverability and self-service** ensure users can find and understand the product through clear descriptions in business language, usage examples, getting-started guides, and readily available support.

- **Continuous evolution** recognizes that successful products evolve based on user feedback, with regular updates, proper version management, and clear deprecation processes when products reach end-of-life.

In summary, a data product is a maintained, governed data asset designed to deliver repeatable value to a specific set of users for a defined business purpose.

Reflection: Think about a data initiative in your organization. How does it measure against these five characteristics?

The Data Product Spectrum

Not all data products are created equal. Understanding where your products fit on the maturity spectrum helps set appropriate expectations and investment levels.

Data Product Maturity Spectrum

Increasing Business Value and Technical Sophistication

Level 1: Basic Data Products

Features:
- Clean, well-structured datasets
- Comprehensive documentation
- Self-service access

Examples:
Customer 360, Financial cubes

Value: Faster access to trusted data

Level 2: Enhanced Analytics

Features:
- Interactive dashboards
- Data exploration tools
- Point-and-click analysis

Examples:
Sales dashboards, Monitoring tools

Value: Insights accessible to all

Level 3: Advanced Algorithmic

Features:
- Machine learning models
- Predictive analytics
- Automated recommendations

Examples:
Fraud detection, Demand forecasting

Value: Automated decision support

Level 4: AI-Powered Systems

Features:
- Real-time AI processing
- Context-aware intelligence
- Self-improving systems

Examples:
Conversational analytics, Agents

Value: Business transformation

Master each level before advancing to the next

Build capabilities incrementally • Focus on business value at every stage

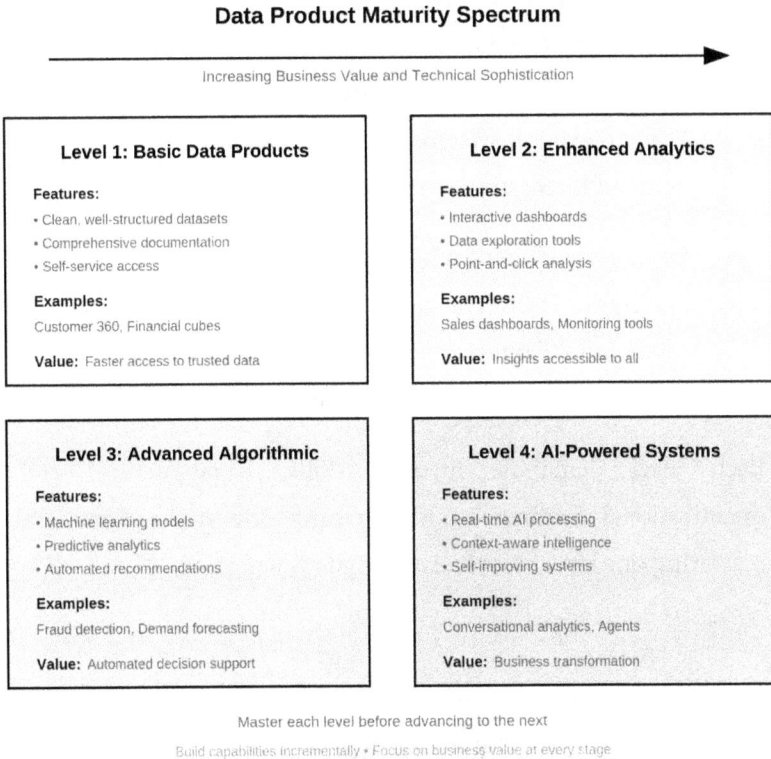

Figure 3: Data Product Maturity Spectrum.

- **Level 1: Basic Data Products** feature clean, documented datasets with basic quality checks. Examples include customer 360 datasets and financial reporting cubes.

- **Level 2: Enhanced Analytics Products** build on this foundation with interactive dashboards and guided exploration capabilities. Sales performance dashboards and operational monitoring tools exemplify this level.

- **Level 3: Advanced Algorithmic Products** introduce machine learning models, recommendations, and predictions embedded directly into business workflows. Fraud detection systems, recommendation engines, and demand forecasting represent this maturity level.

- **Level 4: Intelligent AI--Powered Systems** represent the cutting edge with real-time, context-aware, self-improving capabilities. Conversational analytics, autonomous pricing, and predictive maintenance exemplify this level.

Each level demands different skills, infrastructure, and organizational readiness—and you can't skip stages. Focus on mastering one level before advancing to the next.

Data Mesh versus Non-Data Mesh Approaches

Data mesh has become the hot topic at every data conference, often presented as a magic solution. Let me give you the real story about when it works and when it doesn't.

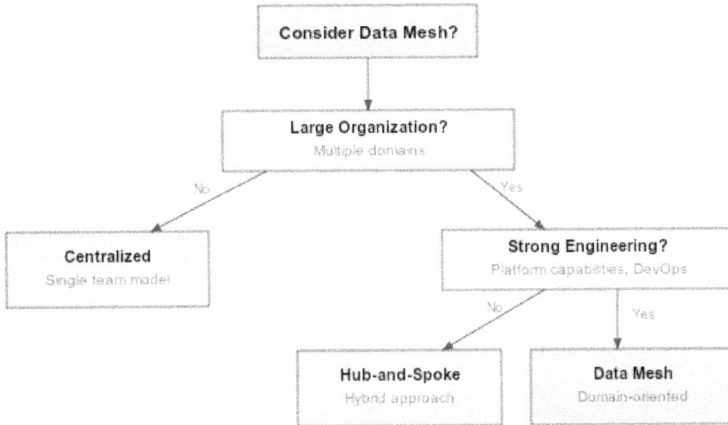

Figure 4: Data Mesh Decision Framework. Choose the model that matches your organizational scale and capabilities.[2]

The Traditional Centralized Approach

Most organizations start with a "hub and spoke" model where a central data team owns everything while business teams submit requests. This creates bottlenecks in which every data request passes through a single team, resulting in delays that stretch for months. The central data team lacks deep domain knowledge, leading to misaligned solutions. One team can't hire fast enough to meet growing demands across all business areas.

---

[2] Data mesh refers to an organizational and architectural approach that emphasizes domain-owned data products with federated governance. Hub-and-spoke models centralize data platforms or teams while distributing access and consumption across domains. Hybrid models combine elements of both, adapting ownership and governance patterns to organizational maturity and constraints.

When Data Mesh Makes Sense

Data mesh works when you have large organizations with distinct business domains, mature technical capabilities distributed across teams, and strong leadership commitment to organizational change. The model requires significant investment in training, tooling, and governance frameworks.

When to Avoid Data Mesh

Skip data mesh if you're a smaller organization with limited technical resources, have simple data needs that don't justify distributed complexity, lack strong governance capabilities, or have leadership that isn't committed to the cultural changes required. I've seen too many organizations attempt data mesh because it sounds modern, only to create chaos without ever seeing the promised benefits.

Mini Case Study: The Insurance Company's Awakening

A mid-sized insurance company began with a typical centralized model in which its 12-person data team handled all requests from underwriting, claims, sales, and finance departments.

The Problem: The data team backlog grew to over 200 items with average wait times exceeding four months. Business teams created shadow analytics using Excel, leading to conflicting numbers in executive meetings.

The Approach: They reorganized around four core data products: Underwriting Risk Analytics, Claims Processing Intelligence, Customer Analytics, and Financial Reporting. Each product had a dedicated product manager who understood both the business domain and user needs. The change was implemented progressively, with early pilots informing broader rollout and adoption.

The Outcome: Once core product ownership and delivery practices were in place, the time to deliver new data capabilities dropped from over four months to a few weeks. The data team backlog went from roughly six months to about two weeks. Quarterly internal surveys measuring satisfaction with data team responsiveness, output quality, and time-to-insight improved from 34 to 87 (on a 100-point scale), and the cost per data request fell from around $2,400 to roughly $180.

They didn't need more data engineers;
they needed product thinking.

The Data Product Lifecycle

Understanding the lifecycle is crucial for managing data products effectively. I use a framework adapted from traditional product management but tailored for data's unique characteristics.

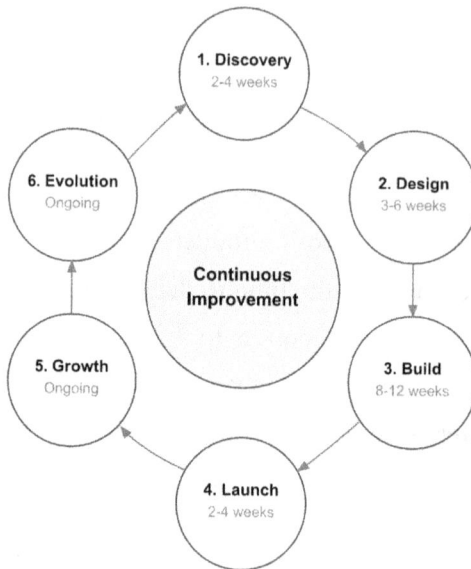

Figure 5: Data Product Lifecycle. Each stage builds on the previous, enabling continuous value delivery.

- **Discovery and Validation** (2-4 weeks) involve identifying business problems, conducting user research, developing value hypotheses, and performing feasibility checks.

- **Design and Architecture** (3-6 weeks) focus on data architecture planning, user experience design, quality requirements definition, and integration point identification.

- **Development and Testing** (8-12 weeks) emphasize iterative development with user feedback, quality assurance implementation, and security and compliance verification.

- **Launch and Adoption** (2-4 weeks) involve pilot testing with power users, comprehensive training and support, and systematic feedback collection.

- **Growth and Optimization** involve ongoing usage analysis, performance optimization, and feature enhancement based on user needs.

- **Maintenance and Evolution** provide ongoing support, data refresh management, and lifecycle decisions regarding enhancements, replacements, or retirements.

Reflection: Map a current data initiative to this lifecycle. What phase are you in? What activities are you missing?

Common Pitfalls and How to Avoid Them

After implementing data products across dozens of organizations, I've seen the same mistakes repeated again and again:

- **Technology-First Thinking** is the most damaging pitfall. Teams build impressive technical architecture without understanding user needs, leading to elegant solutions that solve the wrong problems. Warning signs include architecture diagrams getting more attention than user research and teams talking more about tools than problems. Always start with the business problem and require signed-off business cases before development begins.

- **Assuming Users Will Come** keeps appearing. "If you build it, they will come" doesn't work for data products. You'll notice this when there's no adoption strategy, people assume users will "just discover" the value, and success is measured only with technical metrics. Plan for adoption from day one, including user research, change management, and ongoing support.

- **Ignoring Data Quality** undermines user trust quickly and permanently. This shows up as quality checks bolted on at the end, no clear standards or SLAs, and users discovering errors in published data. Build quality into every pipeline and work with business stakeholders to define acceptable error rates.

- **Poor Documentation and Support** prevent effective utilization. Warning signs include support tickets full of basic "how do I...?" questions and documentation written for technical audiences. Invest in documentation as a product feature, including examples, FAQs, and clear support channels.

- **Lack of Clear Ownership** creates accountability gaps. This appears as unclear accountability for product decisions and no single point of contact for users. Establish clear ownership roles from the beginning.

Building Your Data Product Foundation

Before diving into specific implementation tactics, organizations need strategic clarity through systematic assessment. I recommend conducting a **Five-Foundation Assessment**, rating your organization on each foundation using a 1-5 scale:

- **Strategic Clarity** evaluates whether you have clear business problems that data products should solve, executive sponsorship, and defined success metrics.

- **User Understanding** assesses whether you know who your users are, have conducted user research, and drive product decisions based on user needs.

- **Technical Readiness** examines whether you have the infrastructure to support data products, reliable data sources, and the necessary skills.

- **Organizational Readiness** determines whether teams are organized around user value, have product management capabilities, and embrace a culture of experimentation.

- **Governance Foundation** evaluates whether you have data quality standards, clear policies for data access and security, and processes for managing product lifecycles.

A scoring guide helps interpret results: 20-25 points indicate readiness to build a comprehensive strategy, 15-19 show a strong foundation with some gaps, 10-14 suggest significant work is needed, and under ten means focus on foundational capabilities first.

Reflection: Complete this assessment for your organization. Which foundations need the most attention?

Key Success Factors for Data Products

Over time, I've noticed factors that consistently predict whether data products succeed or fade away.

- **Strong Business Sponsorship** proves essential because you need champions who will advocate for adoption and provide feedback.

- **Clear Value Proposition** ensures users understand "What's in it for me?" This looks like value propositions expressed in business terms, benefits quantified wherever possible, and clear connections between features and business outcomes.

- **Quality and Reliability** form the foundation of user trust. This means automated quality checks in all pipelines, clear SLAs for freshness and accuracy, and quick resolution of quality issues.

- **User-Centric Design** requires designing for actual users, not the data team. Success looks like interfaces designed around user workflows, terminology matching business language, and integration with tools users already use.

- **Continuous Improvement** recognizes that successful products evolve based on feedback. This involves regular user feedback collection, usage analytics, and feature development based on user needs.

The Data Product Charter Template

To operationalize these concepts, I've developed a charter template that forces clear thinking about each data product.

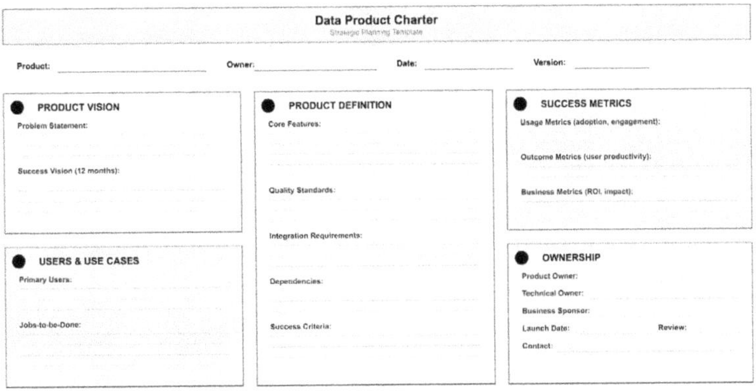

Figure 6: Data Product Charter Template.

- The **Product Vision** section captures the problem statement, success vision, and user impact.

- **Users and Use Cases** identify primary users, specific jobs they're trying to get done, and success criteria.

- **Product Definition** outlines core features, quality standards, and integration requirements.

- **Success Metrics** establishes usage, outcome, and business metrics.

- **Ownership and Operations** assign the product owner, technical owner, and business sponsor.

Looking Forward

This chapter has established the fundamental shift from data projects to data products.

Successful data products need the same discipline and user focus as any other product your company creates. Understanding what data products are is just the beginning. The real challenge lies in organizing teams, implementing governance, measuring value, and scaling across the organization.

The next chapter explores how to organize teams to build and maintain these products effectively, covering the roles needed, how they should work together, and how to structure teams for both centralized and federated approaches.

Key Takeaways

Product thinking changes everything about how we approach data work. When we focus on user problems rather than technical capabilities, we build solutions people actually want to use.

One size doesn't fit all when it comes to organizational models. The choice between centralized, hub-and-spoke, or domain-aligned structures depends on your specific context and maturity level.

Foundation matters more than most people realize. Strong foundations enable successful products and sustainable growth, while weak foundations guarantee struggles regardless of the effort invested later.

Continuous improvement is essential because user needs evolve, business contexts change, and technology capabilities advance. Data products must be designed for evolution.

Your Next Steps

Start by completing the Five-Foundation Assessment to understand your current state and priority improvement areas. Identify one existing data initiative to transform using product principles. Choose something with engaged business stakeholders and clear success criteria. Create a Data Product Charter for that initiative to drive clear thinking about users, value, and success metrics. Begin user research to understand actual needs and pain points rather than making assumptions.

The journey from data projects to data products begins with changing how we think. Master this mindset shift, and everything else becomes possible.

Two

Team Organization for Data Product Success

The Human Side of Data Products

I learned a hard lesson early in my data career: you can build the most elegant data architecture in the world, but if you don't get the people and organization right, it will fail. I've seen $1 million data platforms gather dust because nobody thought about who would use them or how teams would work together.

Data products succeed or fail based on human collaboration, not technical architecture. A mediocre technical solution with great team dynamics will beat brilliant technology with poor collaboration every time.

This chapter is about organizing teams to maximize that collaboration while building products that create genuine business value.

The Traditional Data Team Structure (And Why It Doesn't Scale)

Most companies start with a single data team that handles everything. Data engineers build and maintain pipelines, data analysts create reports and dashboards, data scientists build models, and a data architect may provide oversight. This works fine when you have simple needs and a small user base.

But as your organization becomes more data-driven, this model hits predictable problems. Every data request flows through one team, creating queues that stretch for months. The data team lacks deep domain knowledge about sales, marketing, operations, or customer service, so they build products that are technically correct but miss business nuances. You can't hire data engineers fast enough to keep up with demand. Business stakeholders don't feel responsible for data quality or adoption.

A manufacturing company I worked with had a central data team of six people serving 1,200 employees across four plants. They had 47 active data requests with an average delivery time of eight months. Business stakeholders were building shadow systems in Excel while the data team worked over 60 hours per week. When the finance team built their own monthly reporting system because they couldn't wait, it created conflicting numbers in board presentations. This led to a two-hour executive meeting to figure out why the revenue figures didn't match.

The solution wasn't to hire more data engineers. It was to reorganize around products and users.

The Federated Chaos Alternative

Some organizations swing to the opposite extreme: every department gets its own data resources. This creates different but equally challenging problems. Inconsistent standards emerge when each department chooses its own tools and applies its own quality rules. Duplicated effort wastes resources as multiple teams independently solve the same problems. Integration nightmares develop when getting a company-wide view requires integrating systems that were never designed to work together.

The Data Product Team Model

The solution is to organize around data products rather than technical functions or organizational silos. This doesn't necessarily mean data mesh, as you can apply these principles in centralized organizations too.

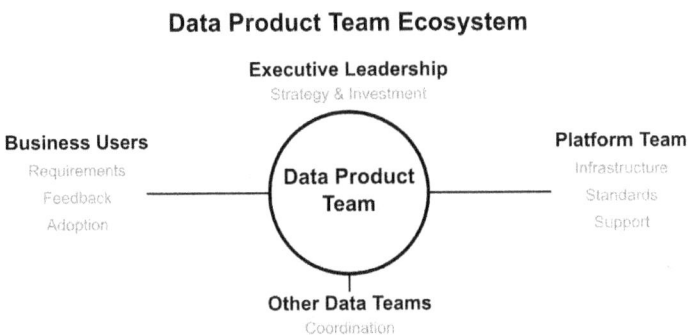

Data Product Team Ecosystem

Executive Leadership
Strategy & Investment

Business Users
Requirements
Feedback
Adoption

Data Product Team

Platform Team
Infrastructure
Standards
Support

Other Data Teams
Coordination

Figure 7: Data Product Team Ecosystem. Teams coordinate around shared data products and business value.

A product-centric organization starts with teams organized around specific data products or user groups rather than technical capabilities. Each team owns its products from conception to retirement, including user adoption and business value creation.

Teams have well-defined ways of working together, with explicit responsibilities and communication protocols. This way of organizing work transforms how teams think about their work.

Instead of being order-takers who respond to requirements, they become product owners who understand user needs and drive business value.

Three Team Topology Options

I've seen three patterns that actually work.

Option 1: Domain-Aligned Data Product Teams (Full Data Mesh)

This is the complete data mesh approach, where each business domain has its own data product team. The team includes a Data Product Manager who owns product strategy and user relationships, Data Engineers who build and maintain pipelines, Data Analysts or Scientists who create analytical products, and a Domain Expert who serves as the business subject matter expert.

This approach works for large organizations with over 1,000 people, distinct business domains with different data needs, mature technical capabilities across the organization, and leadership commitment to significant cultural change.

A major bank reorganized around business domains, creating separate teams for Customer Banking, Investment Services, Risk Management, and Corporate Banking. The reorganization and supporting platform capabilities were rolled out in phases, with early domains piloted before expanding across the organization.

Results after 18 months: Time from idea to data product dropped from six months to six weeks. Business user satisfaction climbed from the low 40s to close to 90%. Data quality incidents fell from around 150 per month to just a dozen. Cross-selling success rates nearly tripled.

Option 2: Hybrid Hub-and-Spoke

A central data platform team provides infrastructure and standards, while domain-specific teams handle products tailored to their business areas. The structure includes a Central Platform Team that provides shared infrastructure, tools, and governance; Domain Data Teams that build products specific to their business areas; and a Center of Excellence that sets standards and shares best practices. This model fits medium-sized organizations that need a balance between consistency and domain autonomy.

An e-commerce company evolved from a centralized to a hybrid structure. Their Central Platform Team provided shared analytics infrastructure and standardized development tools. Domain Teams focused on specialized products. The reorganization and supporting platform capabilities were rolled out in phases, with early domains piloted before expanding across the organization.

Results after 12 months (at steady-state adoption): Platform utilization jumped from roughly a third to over 90%. New product development time dropped from four months to a few weeks. Infrastructure costs fell from $180K to under $100K monthly as legacy pipelines and redundant tooling were progressively retired. The platform was delivered incrementally over a six-month period, starting with a small set of high-impact data products and expanding through thin-slice releases, with adoption increasing as products matured.

Option 3: Product-Focused Central Team

A single data team organized around data products rather than technical functions works for organizations that aren't ready for distributed models. This setup works well for smaller organizations, situations with limited technical resources, environments with strong central leadership, and simpler data landscapes with common user needs.

A healthcare technology startup with 150 employees organized its eight-person data team around products rather than functions.

They created four focused products: Patient Insights, Operational Intelligence, Regulatory Reporting, and Business Intelligence.

Results after nine months: Product adoption rose from the low 20s to nearly 80%. Customer retention moved from the high 60s to the mid-90s, average contract value went from $45K to close to $80K, and team satisfaction scores climbed from six to almost nine out of 10.

Team Organization Models Comparison

Centralized	Hub-and-Spoke	Domain-Aligned
Structure:	**Structure:**	**Structure:**
Single unified team handling all products	Central platform team + domain specialists	Independent teams per business domain
Organization Size:	**Organization Size:**	**Organization Size:**
Small	Medium	Large
Best For:	**Best For:**	**Best For:**
• Simple data needs	• Mixed complexity	• Distinct domains
• Limited resources	• Shared resources	• High autonomy needs
• Strong central control	• Need consistency	• Mature capabilities
Key Trade-off:	**Key Trade-off:**	**Key Trade-off:**
Simple coordination but potential bottleneck	Balanced autonomy with shared efficiency	Maximum autonomy but complex coordination

Figure 8: Team Organization Models Comparison.

Reflection: Which organizational model best fits your current situation? What would need to change to implement it effectively?

Choosing the Right Team Model

Use this simple decision matrix to choose the right team structure:

Factor	Product-Focused Central	Hub-and-Spoke (Hybrid)	Domain-Aligned (Data Mesh)
Organization Size	Small	Medium	Large
Domain Complexity	Simple/Unified	Moderate	High/Distinct
Technical Maturity	Basic	Intermediate	Advanced
Change Readiness	Low	Medium	High
Resource Availability	Limited	Moderate	Abundant

Table 1: Team Structure Decision Matrix.

I would recommend starting with your current organizational capabilities and constraints. Then, choose the model that fits 3+ factors, then evolve gradually toward your target state.

Beyond these core factors, consider geographic distribution, regulatory requirements, existing technical debt, and cultural factors. Organizations with strong collaborative cultures adapt more easily to distributed models, while hierarchical structures may struggle with the autonomy required for domain-aligned teams.

Key Roles and Responsibilities

Regardless of which model you choose, certain roles are essential for data product success.

The Data Product Manager

The Data Product Manager serves as the bridge between business needs and technical implementation, owning product strategy and user relationships. Core responsibilities include conducting user research, defining the product roadmap, managing stakeholder relationships, coordinating with technical teams, measuring product success, and communicating value to leadership. Essential skills include product management fundamentals, business acumen with domain knowledge, technical understanding without coding, stakeholder management, analytical thinking, and project coordination.

The Technical Owner (Data Engineer)

The Technical Owner ensures technical health and reliability, owning infrastructure, pipelines, and technical implementation. Core responsibilities include designing and building data pipelines, ensuring data quality and system reliability, implementing security and governance requirements, optimizing performance, providing technical support, and collaborating with platform teams.

Essential skills include strong engineering capabilities, expertise in data pipeline technologies, knowledge of cloud platforms, understanding of security, proficiency in monitoring tools, and collaboration with non-technical stakeholders.

The Business Owner

The Business Owner provides domain expertise and ensures business value realization, serving as the business champion for product adoption. Core responsibilities include defining business requirements, validating product features, driving adoption within their business area, providing domain expertise, measuring business impact, and funding product development. Essential skills include deep domain knowledge, understanding of business processes, ability to translate business needs into requirements, stakeholder influence, basic understanding of data capabilities, and ability to measure and communicate value.

Role	Core Responsibilities	Key Skills	Success Metrics
Data Product Manager (Strategy & Business)	Product strategy & roadmap; User research & requirements; Stakeholder management; Business case development; Adoption & value tracking	Business acumen; Product management; Data literacy; Communication; User research	User adoption %; Business value ROI; User satisfaction; Time to value; Feature usage
Data Engineer (Technical Implementation)	Pipeline design & development; Data quality implementation; Performance optimization; Infrastructure management; API & integration development	Software engineering; Cloud platforms; Product mindset; API design; DevOps/MLOps	System uptime %; Data quality scores; Performance SLAs; Developer velocity; Issue resolution time
Business Data Owner (Domain Expertise)	Domain expertise & context; Quality standards definition; User advocacy & feedback; Business requirements; Training & change management	Business domain; User empathy; Process knowledge; Stakeholder influence; Change leadership	User engagement; Requirements quality; Training completion; Business impact; User satisfaction

Table 2: Data Product Team Roles and Responsibilities.

Success requires close collaboration between all three roles with clear communication and shared accountability.

Team Interaction Patterns and Coordination

Even autonomous teams need ways to work together effectively. The patterns of interaction between teams often determine whether a product-oriented organization succeeds or fails. Regular coordination prevents teams from working in isolation while preserving autonomy. Weekly Cross-Team Syncs address dependencies and shared challenges. Monthly Product Reviews assess business value and alignment with the roadmap. Quarterly Business Reviews evaluate strategic alignment and team effectiveness. Common coordination failures include teams building incompatible systems, a lack of shared standards, unknowingly duplicating problem-solving, and a lack of end-to-end visibility when issues arise.

The Data Product Operating Model

Successful data product organizations need a comprehensive operating model that defines how decisions get made and work gets coordinated. Clear decision rights prevent confusion and delays. Product-level decisions include feature prioritization (Data Product Manager), technical architecture (Data Engineer with Product Manager input), and quality standards (Business Owner with engineering input).

Platform-level decisions encompass technology standards (Platform Team with domain input) and security policies

(Governance Lead). Enterprise-level decisions involve data strategy (Executive committee) and budget allocation (Finance with data leadership).

Effective communication requires regular, structured rhythms. Daily operations include team standups and issue escalation. Weekly coordination involves cross-team sync meetings and user feedback review. Monthly management encompasses product roadmap reviews and resource planning. The quarterly strategy includes strategic planning and a business value assessment.

> *Clear accountability prevents overlap and ensures nothing falls through the cracks.*

R = Responsible | A = Accountable | C = Consulted | I = Informed

Activity	Product Manager	Data Engineer	Business Owner	Platform Team
Product Strategy	A	C	R	I
Technical Architecture	C	A	I	C
Quality Standards	R	C	A	I
User Training	A	I	R	I
Infrastructure Setup	I	C	I	A

Table 3: RACI Matrix for Data Product Teams.

Making the Transition: A Practical Roadmap

Moving from traditional data team structures to product-oriented teams requires careful planning across multiple phases.

Phase 1: Assessment and Planning (3-6 months)

Current state assessment involves mapping existing capabilities, identifying current products and users, assessing organizational readiness, and documenting current processes. Target state design includes choosing an appropriate team structure, defining clear roles, designing coordination mechanisms, and creating a transition timeline.

Phase 2: Foundation Building (6-12 months)

Capability development focuses on hiring or training data product managers, upskilling engineers in product thinking, establishing business data owner roles, and implementing core platform services. Process implementation includes building feedback processes, establishing governance frameworks, creating training systems, and measuring value.

Phase 3: Scaling and Optimization (12 or more months)

Expansion involves scaling to additional teams and products, optimizing team structures based on learning, maturing governance processes, and building advanced platform capabilities. Continuous improvement implements systematic feedback collection and process optimization based on experience.

Common Transition Pitfalls and Solutions

- **Underestimating cultural change**: Teams often focus on technical aspects and ignore human and cultural challenges. Plan for 18-24 months of cultural evolution, as structures can change in a quarter but mindsets rarely do.

- **Unclear role definitions**: When people don't understand their new roles, confusion and conflict arise. Create detailed role descriptions with specific examples, provide training, and establish clear escalation paths.

- **Insufficient product management skills**: Expecting data engineers to become product managers without training sets them up for failure. Either hire experienced product managers or invest in significant training, including product management fundamentals, user research techniques, business case development, and stakeholder management.

Success Metrics for Team Organization

Track metrics across different dimensions: **Team Health** through employee satisfaction, team autonomy, and collaboration effectiveness. **Product Success** via adoption rates, user satisfaction, time from idea to delivery, and business value delivered. **Organizational Metrics,** including decision-making speed, innovation rate, compliance adherence, and cost per data product. Target benchmarks include team satisfaction above 8.0 out of 10, product adoption above 75% for new products within six months, time-to-value under three months, and business value above three times ROI within 12 months.

Looking Forward

Getting team organization right is foundational to data product success. Teams should be organized around users and value creation, not just technical functions. Regardless of the model you choose, certain principles apply: clear ownership and accountability, user-focused product thinking, cross-functional collaboration, and continuous learning and improvement.

The next chapter dives deep into governance models. We'll explore how to balance autonomy with consistency, implement adequate quality controls, and build governance systems that enable rather than constrain teams.

Key Takeaways

Team structure drives culture, and how you organize teams shapes how they think and work. Getting this right from the beginning is easier than trying to fix it later.

Product thinking requires new roles, and data product managers are essential for success. This isn't just a title change; it requires fundamentally different skills and approaches than traditional data roles. One size doesn't fit all organizations. Choose team models based on your context and constraints rather than following the latest trend. Change takes time, so plan for 18-24 months of cultural and organizational evolution. Technical changes happen quickly, but people and process changes require patience and persistence.

Your Next Steps

Begin by assessing your current team structure against the decision matrix to understand where you are and where you need to go. Identify the biggest gaps in roles and skills, particularly around product management capabilities. Design your target team structure for your specific context, accounting for size, complexity, and maturity. Create a 12-month transition plan with specific milestones and success criteria. Most importantly, begin developing or hiring data product management capabilities. This role is often the bottleneck for successful transformation.

There's no perfect team structure, only structures that fit some contexts better than others. Start from where you are, define where you want to go, and plan a gradual transition that builds both capabilities and confidence.

THREE

Governance Models That Enable, Not Constrain

Beyond the Data Police

When I mention "data governance" in workshops, people's energy drain from the room. They think about compliance frameworks, endless documentation, and rigid approval processes that turn two-week projects into two-month bureaucratic marathons. But good governance is invisible to users. It enables teams to move faster and with more confidence. Bad governance is a bottleneck that teams work around, creating more problems than it solves.

> *If teams work around governance, governance is the problem.*

This chapter is about building governance that works in the real world of data products.

The Governance Paradox

There's a fundamental tension in data product organizations: teams need autonomy to move quickly and serve their users, but organizations need consistency, quality, and compliance. Traditional governance tries to solve this with centralized control, but that approach doesn't scale.

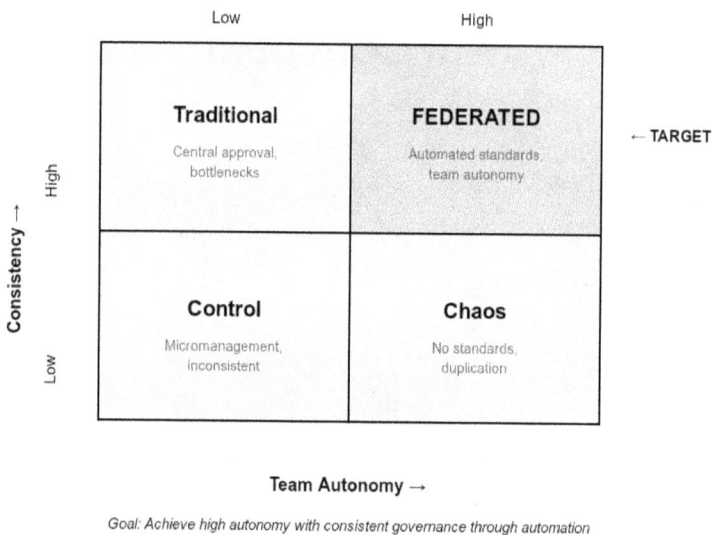

Figure 9: Tension Between Autonomy and Consistency.

I call this the "governance paradox": the more governance you need, the less traditional governance works. Most organizations get stuck trying to control everything from the center and then wonder why nobody follows the rules.

Central approval processes become chokepoints as the number of teams and products grows. I worked with one financial services company that had a 47-step approval process for new data projects. Teams spent more time on governance documentation than on product development. Central teams lack domain expertise to make good decisions about specific products. Innovation suffers when rigid standards prevent teams from adopting new tools and approaches. Perhaps most damaging is the compliance theater problem, where teams focus on checking boxes rather than delivering actual value.

The Federated Governance Alternative

The solution is federated governance: push governance decisions and responsibilities to the teams closest to the work, while maintaining central standards and oversight. This approach works because teams have the context to make good decisions, governance becomes embedded in daily work rather than serving as external overhead, and organizations can scale without creating bottlenecks.

The Shift Left Philosophy

"Shift left" means moving governance decisions earlier in the product development lifecycle, ideally into the tools and processes teams use every day. Traditional "shift right" governance builds the product first, then applies governance checks at the end. This approach is expensive and often ineffective because problems are harder to fix after they're embedded in systems.

Traditional "Shift Right" Governance

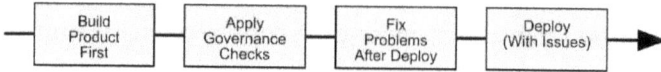

| Build Product First | Apply Governance Checks | Fix Problems After Deploy | Deploy (With Issues) |

Problems: Expensive fixes • Late discovery • User frustration

Modern "Shift Left" Governance

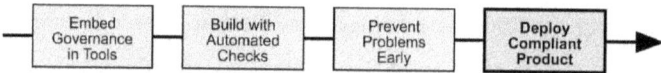

| Embed Governance in Tools | Build with Automated Checks | Prevent Problems Early | **Deploy Compliant Product** |

Benefits: Early detection • Lower costs • Better user experience

Shift governance left to prevent problems, not just find them

Figure 10: Shift Reft versus Shift Light Governance.

"Shift left" governance embeds governance into development tools, provides automated checks and guidance, and prevents problems from occurring. Instead of submitting a data product for privacy review after it's built, the development platform automatically scans for PII data as the product is created, flags potential issues, and provides guidance on proper handling.

Reflection: Think about your current governance processes. How much time is spent on post-deployment fixes versus prevention?

The Four-Layer Governance Stack

I think about governance as a stack with four layers, each serving different purposes and requiring different implementation approaches.

HUMAN	**Layer 4** **Strategic** **Oversight**	**Strategic Direction** • Governance councils and executive oversight • Policy setting and risk management	**10% effort**
	Layer 3 **Process &** **Controls**	**Human Judgment** • Manual reviews and exception handling • Data classification and access management	**20% effort**
AUTOMATED	**Layer 2** **Computational** **Policies**	**Automated Rules** • Policy as code and quality gates • Automated validation and access controls	**30% effort**
	Layer 1 **Infrastructure** **Automation**	**Built-in Governance** • Auto-cataloging and quality monitoring • Infrastructure as code, security by default	**40% effort**

> **Investment Principle: Focus 70% of effort on automation layers**
> Keep oversight layers lightweight • Build governance into tools, not processes

Figure 11: Four-Layer Governance Stack.

The foundation layer focuses on **Infrastructure Automation** that embeds governance into the platform itself. This includes automatic data cataloging, continuous quality monitoring, and infrastructure-as-code that ensures consistent, compliant deployments. When governance is built into the infrastructure, teams get compliance benefits without additional effort.

The second layer involves **Computational Policies**, in which governance rules are expressed as executable code. Policy as code enables automated enforcement, quality gates prevent bad data from entering systems, and access controls ensure security and compliance. This layer makes governance consistent and scalable while reducing the burden on human reviewers.

The third layer addresses **Process and Controls** that handle scenarios requiring human judgment. Data classification and access management provide structure, quality standards give teams clear guidance, and manual reviews address edge cases that automation can't resolve. This layer balances automation with human oversight.

The top layer provides **Strategic Oversight** through governance councils that set the overall direction. Policy setting and dispute resolution ensure consistent application of governance principles, while strategic alignment connects governance to business objectives. This layer provides direction and accountability without micromanaging daily operations.

Most effort should go into the bottom layers (automated controls and standards). The top layers should be lightweight monitoring rather than heavy-handed control.

Layer 1: Automated Controls (Platform Level)

This layer represents governance built into the tools teams use daily. Automatic data classification and tagging discover and label data based on content without manual effort. Built-in encryption and access controls protect sensitive information by default. Automated quality checks identify issues immediately when they occur. For example, a data platform automatically detects credit card numbers and applies appropriate security controls without any manual intervention. The system recognizes patterns, applies encryption, restricts access, and logs all interactions, ensuring compliance happens naturally as part of normal operations.

Start with high-risk, high-volume scenarios where automation provides the greatest benefit. Build detection rules into data ingestion pipelines to catch problems at the source. Provide automatic remediation where possible, and alert humans only for edge cases that require judgment.

Layer 2: Standards and Templates (Process Level)

This layer provides standardized approaches that teams can easily adopt and customize. Data product templates give teams proven starting points rather than blank slates. Quality testing templates offer pre-built checks for common scenarios. Documentation standards ensure consistency without requiring extensive training. A data product canvas guides teams through key governance considerations during product design, making compliance a natural part of the design process rather than an afterthought. Teams start with a template that prompts them to consider privacy, security, quality, and user needs from the beginning.

Success factors include making templates opinionated but flexible, providing examples and best practices, making it easier to do the right thing than the wrong thing, and implementing regular updates based on user feedback.

Computational Governance

Computational governance means encoding governance rules into automated systems. Instead of relying on humans to remember and apply governance requirements, we build them into the tools and processes.

Data Classification and Tagging

Automatic identification and labeling of data based on content and context reduces manual effort while improving consistency. The technical implementation uses pattern matching for PII, machine learning models trained on sample data, context-aware classification based on source systems, and integration with existing data catalogs. For example, a financial services company implemented automated PII detection, reducing manual classification effort by over 95% while improving accuracy from 78% to above 99%.

Policy as Code Implementation

Governance policies expressed as executable code enable consistent, scalable enforcement. Example policies might require PII data encryption at rest with automatic enforcement, financial data approval for external sharing with workflow enforcement, and data retention rules that automatically archive or delete data older than specified periods. This involves integration with CI/CD Continuous Integration/Continuous Deployment) pipelines for automatic policy checking, runtime policy enforcement in data processing systems, API gateways that enforce access policies, and automated remediation for policy violations.

Reflection: What governance decisions in your organization are currently manual? Which ones could be automated with the right tools and processes?

Building a Governance Operating Model

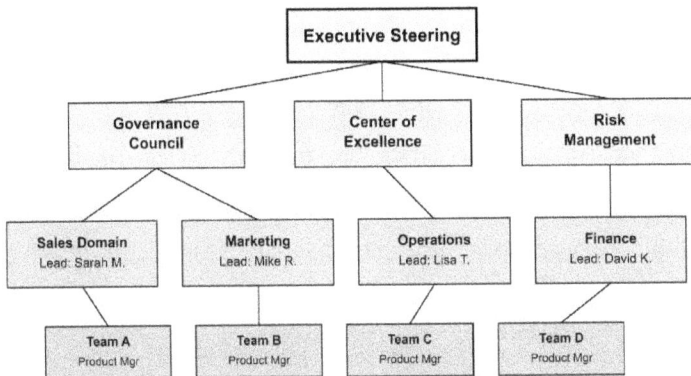

Figure 12: Governance Operating Model.

Successful governance needs more than just technology. It demands an operating model that defines roles, responsibilities, and processes.

The Governance Council Model

A cross-functional council sets standards and resolves escalations while maintaining business focus. Council composition includes representatives from major business domains, data platform and engineering leadership, legal, compliance, and risk management, security and privacy specialists, and external stakeholders as needed.

Council responsibilities include setting enterprise-wide governance standards, resolving cross-domain governance conflicts, reviewing and approving major governance changes, monitoring governance effectiveness, and communicating governance updates across the organization.

The meeting structure includes monthly standard business meetings to review metrics and address escalations, emergency sessions to address critical compliance issues, and quarterly strategic reviews to assess governance effectiveness.

Domain Governance Leads

Each domain or product team designates a governance lead who serves as the bridge between the team and organizational governance. Their job involves implementing governance standards within their domain, serving as liaison to the governance council, providing governance training to team members, monitoring compliance and quality metrics, and escalating issues that require council attention.

The ideal profile is a senior technical person with domain expertise who can influence team behavior and has credibility with both technical and business stakeholders. Success factors include allocating 20-30% of time to governance activities, direct access to the governance council, and authority to make day-to-day governance decisions.

Center of Excellence Structure

A small central team supports governance across the organization without becoming a bottleneck. Team composition includes governance specialists with deep technical and regulatory knowledge, data architects who understand the enterprise data landscape, training and communication specialists, and tool specialists who can implement automated governance.

Team responsibilities involve developing governance standards and templates, providing consultation and training services, implementing and maintaining governance tooling, monitoring enterprise-wide compliance, and researching new governance approaches.

Data Quality as a Governance Foundation

Data quality is fundamentally a governance challenge. Poor quality data undermines trust in all data products and creates compliance risks.

Quality Dimensions and Standards

Completeness standards might require 95% of records to have all mandatory fields populated. We measure this by tracking the percentage of records with missing critical fields, automate it by flagging incomplete records, and the business impact appears when incomplete customer records hurt marketing effectiveness.

For accuracy, we typically demand 99% of customer contact information be correct. We measure through error rates from validation checks and user feedback, automate via address validation and format checking, and the business impact shows up as failed deliveries and frustrated customers when data is inaccurate.

Consistency means customer data matches across all systems. We measure by looking at records with conflicts between systems, automate using cross-system validation rules, and the business impact shows up as customer service problems when data doesn't match.

Quality Monitoring Framework

Continuous monitoring involves automatically running quality checks across all pipelines. Exception handling includes clear processes for handling quality issues, including the automatic quarantine of bad data and escalation procedures.

Root cause analysis provides a systematic investigation to prevent recurrence, not just fix immediate issues. Quality reporting gives regular reporting on quality metrics in a business language, connecting data quality to business outcomes.

A retail company's marketing team defined "good" customer data as complete contact information, accurate demographic data verified within 90 days, purchase history within two years, and valid loyalty program status. The technical team implemented automated checks to address these requirements, while the marketing team remained accountable for defining standards and resolving quality issues.

Common Governance Pitfalls

Understanding common failures helps organizations avoid expensive mistakes.

Governance Theater

This occurs when impressive-looking governance processes don't actually improve outcomes. Warning signs include focus on documentation rather than results, compliance metrics that don't correlate with business outcomes, and teams spending more time on governance than on productive work.

Focus on metrics that matter to business outcomes.

Measure governance effectiveness by business impact, not process completion. Connect governance activities directly to business value and user satisfaction.

Over-Engineering

Building complex governance systems that are difficult to use creates more problems than it solves. Warning signs include governance tools that require extensive training, simple decisions that require complex approval processes, and teams that actively work around governance systems.

Start simple and evolve based on actual needs. Build governance into existing workflows rather than creating parallel processes.

Focus on solving real problems
rather than theoretical edge cases.

Lack of Business Buy-In

When governance is seen as an IT initiative rather than a business necessity, it fails to address real business risks. Warning signs include business stakeholders not participating in governance decisions, governance standards that don't reflect business priorities, and compliance issues that surprise business leadership.

Connect governance directly to business risk and value. Show how governance enables better decision-making and prevents business problems. Include business stakeholders in the design and implementation of governance.

Reflection: Which of these pitfalls does your organization face? What specific steps could you take to address the most critical ones?

Your Governance Transformation Roadmap

This is a practical approach to building governance capabilities that scales with your organization and contains four phases:

- **Phase 1, Foundation (Months 1-6)**: Establish an operating model by forming a governance council with business representation, clearly defining roles and responsibilities, and establishing escalation paths. Implement basic automation, starting with high-value, low-complexity tasks. Next, implement data classification and quality monitoring, and create initial standards and templates. Pilot with high-value use cases by choosing two to three products with engaged business stakeholders.

- **Phase 2, Automation (Months 6-12)**: Expand automated controls by implementing automated policy checking and enforcement, building governance into development tools, and expanding quality monitoring. Scale across products by applying learnings from pilots to additional products, developing governance as a service for product teams, and adding privacy and compliance automation. Whether implemented through data mesh, hub-and-spoke, or hybrid models, the core requirement remains clear ownership paired with federated governance.

- **Phase 3, AI Integration (Months 12-18)**: Detailed AI governance implementation will be covered extensively in Chapter 6, including bias detection, model monitoring, and explainable AI requirements.

- **Phase 4, Optimization (Months 18 and beyond)**: Continuous improvement involves advanced analytics on governance metrics, machine learning for quality monitoring, and self-service governance tools. Strategic integration includes full integration with business processes and governance as a competitive advantage.

Key Takeaways

Governance should enable, not constrain, making teams more confident and productive rather than slower. The more governance you can embed in tools and processes, the less overhead it creates for teams.

Start with business value by connecting governance directly to business outcomes and risk management. Show how good governance prevents problems and enables better decision-making. Build incrementally, starting with basic capabilities and evolving based on real-world feedback. Perfect governance systems don't exist, but systems that solve real problems create tremendous value. Make governance invisible at build time by embedding it so deeply into workflows that teams don't have to think about compliance mechanics, while still making outcomes, decisions, and limitations explicit and understandable to users and stakeholders. The best governance feels like a natural part of getting work done.

Focus on culture because governance is ultimately about building a culture of responsibility and quality. Technology and processes support this culture, but they can't replace it.

Your Next Steps

Begin by assessing your current governance maturity using the four-layer model to identify gaps and opportunities. Identify the biggest governance pain points in your organization through interviews with teams and business stakeholders.

Choose one high-impact area for automation, such as data classification or quality monitoring, where you can demonstrate immediate value. Form a governance council with real business representation, not just technical members.

Begin planning for AI governance requirements, as these will become increasingly important regardless of your current AI adoption level. The organizations that prepare now will have significant advantages as AI becomes more prevalent.

Once governance is clear, the next step is to connect everything you're doing to measurable business value. Governance gives you the rules of the game; value tells you whether you're winning.

FOUR

Data Product Value Chain and Business Impact

The Million-Dollar Question

"What's the ROI of this data initiative?" I hear this question in every C-suite presentation, and it used to make me cringe. Early in my career, I'd mumble something about "better decision-making" and "improved insights" while executives exchanged skeptical glances. I was talking about data; they were thinking about dollars. Once I understood that mismatch and learned to speak their language, everything about how I framed value had to change. Data products aren't valuable because they're technically impressive—they're valuable when they solve real business problems and create measurable impact. This chapter is about understanding, measuring, and communicating that value in terms that drive investment and support.

The Data Value Chain: From Raw Material to Business Impact

Data becomes valuable when it's transformed into products that drive business decisions and actions. Most organizations think about data value linearly: collect data, store it, process it, analyze it, then act. This model isn't wrong, but it's incomplete. It focuses on moving data around instead of creating value.

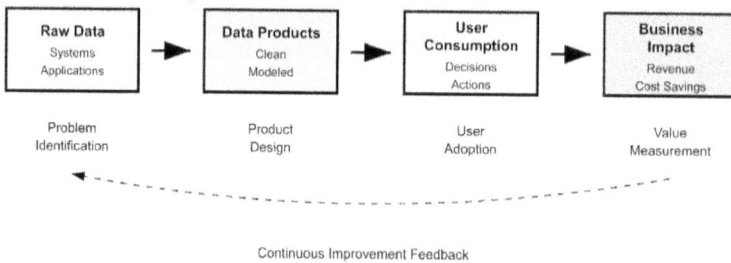

Figure 13: Data Product Value Chain.

A product-oriented approach views value creation and capture differently. The value chain starts with raw data from systems and applications, transforms it through cleaning, aggregation, and modeling into data products. Users then consume these products to make decisions, take actions, and automate workflows.

> Business impact is realized through increased revenue, reduced costs, and improved efficiency.

The process flow looks fundamentally different from traditional approaches. Instead of starting with data collection, we begin with problem identification, conduct user research, design products, build solutions, drive adoption, measure value, and evolve continuously. Notice the difference: we start with business problems and end with business impact.

If value can't be explained, it can't be defended.

Data engineering is important, but it's in service of business value, not an end in itself.

Value Creation versus Value Capture

Value creation represents the actual business benefit generated by the data product, while value capture reflects the organization's ability to measure and realize that benefit. You can create tremendous value without measuring it. A recommendation engine might improve customer satisfaction and retention, but if you can't measure those improvements, you can't prove the system's value or justify continued investment.

A telecommunications company built a sophisticated network optimization system that reduced dropped calls by 23%. The system worked perfectly from a technical perspective, but nobody connected the improvement to the data product. Customer service complaints decreased, but that was attributed to network infrastructure improvements. Only after implementing proper attribution tracking did they realize the optimization system was generating $2.4 million in retained revenue annually.

Value without measurement is invisible value.

Reflection: Think about a recent data initiative in your organization. Can you clearly connect it to specific business outcomes?

Understanding Business Value Types

Not all business value looks the same. I categorize data product value into four types, each with different characteristics and measurement approaches.

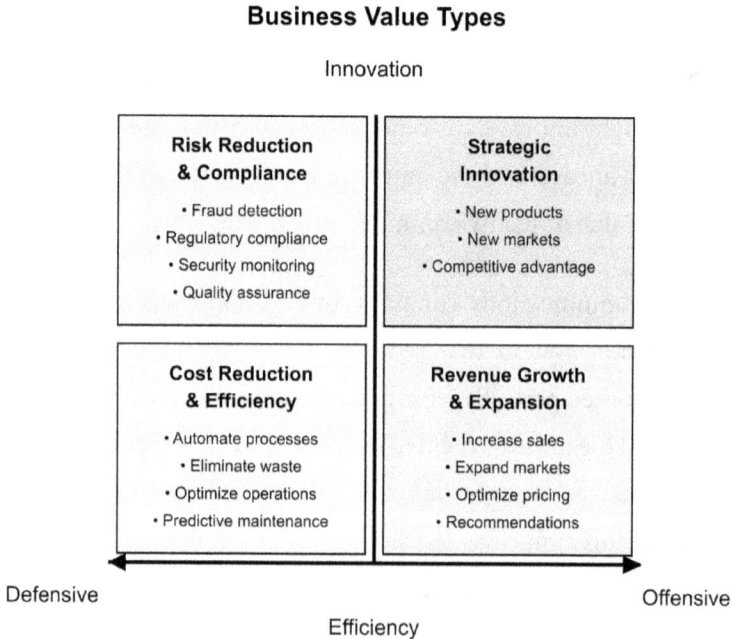

Business Value Types

Innovation

Risk Reduction & Compliance	Strategic Innovation
• Fraud detection • Regulatory compliance • Security monitoring • Quality assurance	• New products • New markets • Competitive advantage
Cost Reduction & Efficiency	**Revenue Growth & Expansion**
• Automate processes • Eliminate waste • Optimize operations • Predictive maintenance	• Increase sales • Expand markets • Optimize pricing • Recommendations

Defensive ⟷ Offensive

Efficiency

Figure 14: Business Value Types.

Type 1: Cost Reduction and Efficiency

This is often the easiest value to measure and most compelling because the benefits are direct and quantifiable. Examples include automating manual reporting, predictive maintenance to reduce downtime, fraud detection to prevent losses, and supply chain optimization to reduce inventory costs.

A retail company's HR team spent 20 hours per month manually creating hiring reports. We automated this with a data product that took two hours to set up and ran automatically. Benefits include 18 hours saved monthly (216 hours annually) at $65 per hour, which generated $14,040 in annual cost savings, plus improved accuracy and timeliness.

Type 2: Revenue Generation and Growth

While harder to measure directly, revenue impact is often more valuable than cost savings. Examples include recommendation engines increasing average order value, customer segmentation improving marketing ROI, and price optimization maximizing revenue. Measurement uses A/B testing, cohort analysis, and attribution modeling.

An e-commerce client implemented a recommendation system that increased average order value by 12%. At $50M in annual revenue, that's $6M in additional revenue. Even if you only attribute 50% to the recommendation system, you still get roughly $3M in value.

Type 3: Risk Reduction and Compliance

Often undervalued until something goes wrong, risk reduction creates significant value by preventing problems. Examples include compliance monitoring to prevent regulatory fines, risk scoring to reduce bad debt, and security analytics to detect threats faster.

A financial services client faced potential GDPR fines of up to $40M. Our privacy compliance data product costs $500K annually. With a 15% annual probability of violation and a potential $40M fine, the expected annual loss was $6M. The net value was $5.5M annually.

Type 4: Strategic Capabilities and Options

The hardest to quantify but potentially most valuable long-term, strategic capabilities create options for future value creation. Examples include customer data platforms enabling personalization at scale, unified data foundations supporting new product development, real-time infrastructure opening new market opportunities, and AI-ready architectures accelerating time-to-market. Measurement uses option valuation: probability-weighted expected value of enabled initiatives. At one client, we built a customer data platform that didn't generate immediate ROI but created options: personalization engine (expected value: $2M, probability: 70%), real-time recommendations ($1.5M, 60%), and predictive analytics ($1M, 80%). Total option value: $3.1M against $1M platform cost.

Comprehensive Value Measurement Framework

I use a three-level metrics hierarchy that connects activity to impact. Most dashboards fail because they measure activity rather than value:

- **Level 1: Usage Metrics (Activity)** indicate adoption but don't guarantee value creation: number of users, data volume processed, API calls, time spent in product.

- **Level 2: Outcome Metrics (Effectiveness)** show the product is working as intended: user productivity improvements, decision-making speed, process automation, and user satisfaction.

- **Level 3: Impact Metrics (Business Value)** connect products to business outcomes, including revenue impact, cost savings, risk reduction, and competitive advantage.

Most organizations focus too heavily on Level 1 metrics. High usage doesn't guarantee business value. Connect usage to outcomes and outcomes to impact.

ROI Calculation Frameworks

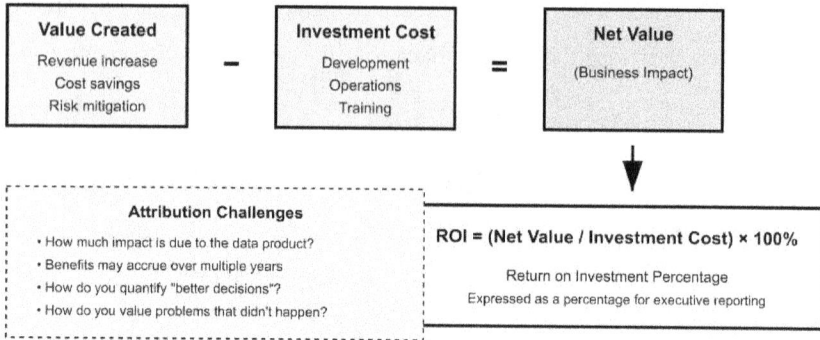

Figure 15: ROI Calculation Flow.

The basic ROI formula is simple in theory, complex in practice:

ROI = (Value Created - Cost of Investment) / Cost of Investment × 100%

Challenges include value attribution, time horizons, intangible benefits, and avoided costs.

Framework 1: The Value Driver Tree

Break down business value into specific, measurable components that can be tracked and attributed.

For a Customer Churn Prediction System, the primary value driver is reduced customer churn with three sub-drivers:

- Earlier customer identification increases the prediction lead time from 30 to 90 days.

- An improved marketing retention campaign effectiveness increases the retention rate from 65% to 75%.

- Better resource allocation improves retention ROI by 20%.

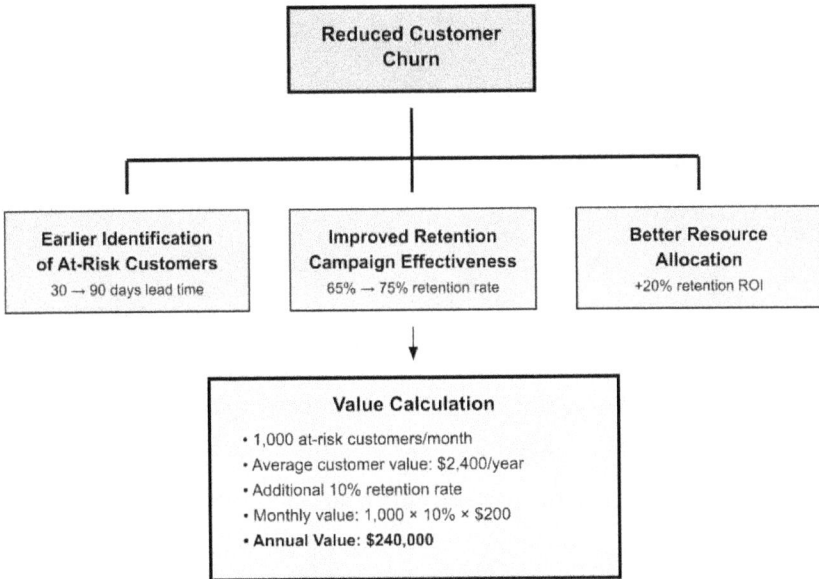

Figure 16: Customer Churn Prediction Value Driver Tree.

The calculation: 1,000 at-risk customers per month, with an average customer value of $2,400 annually. An additional 10% retention rate generates a monthly value of 1,000 × 10% × $2,400/12 = $20,000, for a total of $240,000 in annual value.

Framework 2: The Comparison Approach

Compare data-driven approaches to alternative solutions. Manual fraud detection catches 60% of fraud, basic analytics 75%, and an

ML solution 90%. With $5M in potential fraud annually, the status quo prevents $3M, and an ML solution prevents $4.5M. Additional value: $1.5M annually. With an ML solution costing $400K annually, the net value was $1.1M annually.

Framework 3: The Business Case Template

For executive presentations, structure your story with an **Executive Summary** that captures the problem, solution, investment, return, and timeline. For example, "Our customer service team can't quickly access customer information during calls, leading to 45-second average hold times and 23% call escalation rates. A Customer 360 dashboard that provides real-time customer context will reduce time spent searching for information. Investment of $180K over 12 months will generate $520K annually. Without this, customer satisfaction scores will continue declining, leading to an estimated $1.2M annual churn."

Building Compelling Business Cases

Numbers tell you what happened;
stories tell you why it matters.

Effective business cases combine quantitative analysis with a narrative structure. The challenge paints a picture: "Our call center agents spend 30% of their time looking for customer information across eight different systems, while customers wait on hold." The solution explains how technology addresses this: "Our Customer 360 dashboard provides a single view of each customer with real-time data integration." The impact quantifies results: "This reduces average call time by two minutes, saving $400K annually while improving customer satisfaction scores by 15%."

ROI Sensitivity Analysis

Always test your assumptions with scenarios:

- **Conservative scenario**: 50% of expected benefits, 25% cost overrun, 6-month delay.

- **Expected scenario**: Full benefits, budget on target, timeline as planned.

- **Optimistic scenario**: 125% benefits, 10% cost savings, accelerated benefits.

Sample analysis:

- **Conservative**: $300K benefits, $225K costs, 133% ROI, 18-month payback.

- **Expected**: $600K benefits, $180K costs, 333% ROI, 9-month payback.

- **Optimistic**: $750K benefits, $162K costs, 463% ROI, 6-month payback.

Value Communication Strategies

Know Your Audience

- **CFOs and Financial Leadership** focus on ROI, payback period, and cash flow. Use financial language, detailed cost-benefit analysis, and risk-adjusted returns.

- **Operational Leadership** emphasizes efficiency gains and process improvements. Show before-and-after comparisons, quantify time savings, and highlight customer impact.

- **The board and CEO** focus on strategic impact and competitive advantage. Connect to the company mission, show market positioning, and keep it high-level but substantive.

The Value Dashboard

I use an executive "value dashboard" that gives ongoing visibility into how data products are performing:

- **Real-time ROI tracking** shows current ROI across all products, trending performance, and comparison to projections.

- **Key Business Metrics Impact** displays revenue influenced, cost reductions achieved, and customer satisfaction improvements.

- **User Adoption and Satisfaction** tracks usage rates, satisfaction scores, and support trends.

Mini Case Study: The Retail Analytics Transformation

A regional retail chain with 45 stores was struggling with inventory management and markdown optimization.

The Problem: Manual inventory decisions led to 23% overstock and 18% stockouts. Markdown decisions were made by gut feel. Each store manager used different approaches. Corporate headquarters had no visibility into store-level performance.

The Approach: Three data products addressed these challenges: Inventory Intelligence provided real-time optimization recommendations; Markdown Optimizer delivered data-driven markdown recommendations; and the Store Performance Dashboard provided executives with visibility across all locations.

Metric	Before	After	Impact	Value
Overstock	23%	11%	-12%	$890K
Stockouts	18%	8%	-10%	$1.2M
Markdown efficiency	67%	89%	+22%	$650K
Inventory turns	4.2x	6.1x	+45%	$1.8M

Total Annual Value: $4.54M | **Investment**: $680K | **ROI**: 668% | **Payback Period**: ~6 months (based on phased rollout and gradual value realization)

Table 4: Outcomes after 12 months of incremental rollout and adoption.

Note: Value realization ramped over time as products were deployed and adopted; annual figures reflect steady-state impact rather than first-month returns.

Key success factors included clear baseline measurement, conservative attribution (50% of improvements), multiple measurement methods, and regular communication.

Common Value Measurement Pitfalls

- **Vanity metrics**: Teams measure activity instead of impact, focusing on impressive-sounding numbers that don't connect to business value. Warning signs: "Our dashboard has 10,000 views per month!" These may indicate technical success, but don't demonstrate business value. Instead of dashboard views, measure "Dashboard users make decisions 50% faster."

- **Attribution confusion**: Teams claim credit for business improvements with multiple causes, leading to inflated ROI claims. Use rigorous attribution methods: A/B testing, regression analysis, incremental lift measurements, and conservative attribution. When in doubt, give the product less credit, not more.

- **Cherry-picking results**: Teams report only positive outcomes while ignoring failures. Balanced scorecards work better when they include successful and unsuccessful products, leading and lagging indicators, and risk assessments.

- **Ignoring total cost of ownership**: Teams focus only on development costs while ignoring ongoing operational costs. Full lifecycle cost analysis includes development, operations, training, infrastructure, and opportunity costs. You might spend $180K building the product in year one. Then add infrastructure costs growing from $60K to $86K over three years, plus operations costs increasing from $45K to $65K. Suddenly, your three-year total is around $609K, which is very different from the neat $180K on the original slide.

Looking Forward

Understanding and measuring value is crucial, but it's just the foundation. The real challenge lies in creating products that people actually want to use and building sustainable data product organizations.

The next chapter explores the human side of data product management, like how to conduct user research, design for adoption, and build products that solve real problems for real people.

Key Takeaways

Start with business problems, not data capabilities. Value comes from solving real challenges rather than having impressive technology. Measure what matters by focusing on business impact metrics rather than just usage statistics. High dashboard views don't guarantee business value. They connect usage to outcomes and outcomes to business impact. Build attribution and communication from the beginning: design tracking alongside features, and translate results into business language, including revenue, cost, risk, and competitive advantage.

Be honest about uncertainty using ranges and scenarios rather than false precision. Track the full value chain from raw data to business impact.

Your Next Steps

Choose one data product and create a value driver tree that breaks down its business impact into measurable components. This often reveals gaps in current measurement approaches.

Implement baseline measurement before your next product launch to enable proper before-and-after comparison. Develop a value dashboard for executive communication that connects data product activities to business outcomes in real-time. Train your team to calculate ROI and develop business cases so they can speak the language of business stakeholders.

Numbers inform, but stories persuade. Master both the measurement and the storytelling if you want sustainable support for your data product initiatives.

FIVE

Human-Centric
Data Product Management

The User Problem We Keep Ignoring

I was once asked to diagnose why a "state-of-the-art" data platform had failed. The technology was genuinely impressive: real-time streaming, advanced analytics, machine learning capabilities, and visualizations that belonged in a design museum. But usage was catastrophically low. Less than 8% of intended users logged in regularly, and those who did stayed for an average of 90 seconds.

The problem wasn't technical. The platform worked exactly as designed. The problem was that nobody had talked to users about what they actually needed.

Assumptions scale faster than understanding.

Technical excellence means nothing if humans can't or won't use your product. This chapter is about putting humans at the center of data product design and management.

The biggest mistake data teams make is skipping user research. We assume we understand what people need because we understand data. This assumption is expensive and usually wrong.

The Jobs-To-Be-Done Framework

When users "hire" your data product, what job are they trying to get done? Nobody wakes up excited to run SQL queries. They wake up with business problems to solve.

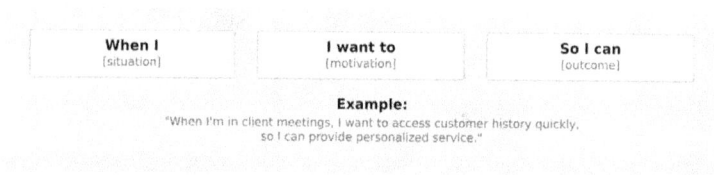

When I	I want to	So I can
[situation]	[motivation]	[outcome]

Example:
"When I'm in client meetings, I want to access customer history quickly, so I can provide personalized service."

Figure 17: Job-To-Be-Done Template.

The job statement template provides structure: "When I [situation], I want to [motivation], so I can [expected outcome]." This format forces clarity about context, need, and success criteria. Real examples from my work:

- "When I'm on a sales call with a prospect, I want to quickly understand their business challenges so that I can position our solution effectively."

- "When I'm planning next quarter's inventory, I want to predict demand accurately so that I can avoid stockouts without excess inventory."

- "When our system performance degrades, I want to identify the root cause immediately, so I can restore service before customers are affected."

Reflection: Write job statements for the primary users of your current data products. Are your products actually designed to help users accomplish these jobs?

User Research Techniques for Data Products

User research for data products needs a different toolkit because data creates its own special confusion for users. Users often can't articulate their data needs clearly, and their stated preferences may differ from actual behavior. They'll tell you they want "all the data," then only ever use two charts.

Structured User Interviews

I conduct structured interviews with five to ten people from each key user group, using a framework specifically designed for data products.

Start with **background questions** about their role and typical workday to understand context.

Move into **current state exploration**: How do they make decisions related to their domain today? What data do they look at regularly and where do they find it? What's their typical workflow? What frustrates them most about current data access?

Explore the **desired state**. What would make their job easier or more effective? What decisions do they wish they could make faster or with more confidence? What questions can't they answer today that they wish they could?

Understanding **context and constraints** always surprises me. How much time do they typically have for analysis? What's their technical comfort level? Who else is involved in these decisions? What happens if they make the wrong decision?

One interview insight demonstrates the power of this approach. A marketing manager told me, "I don't need to know our customer lifetime value down to the penny. I need to know if it's getting better or worse than last month, and I need to know in 30 seconds or less." This single insight reshaped how we designed their analytics product.

Observational Research

Day-in-the-Life Studies involve shadowing users for a full workday to understand their work environment reality. These studies reveal what data they actually look at versus what they say, how much time they spend finding data versus analyzing it, what interrupts their workflow, how they collaborate with others around data, and what manual workarounds they've created.

Journey Mapping captures the complete user experience from problem identification to action.

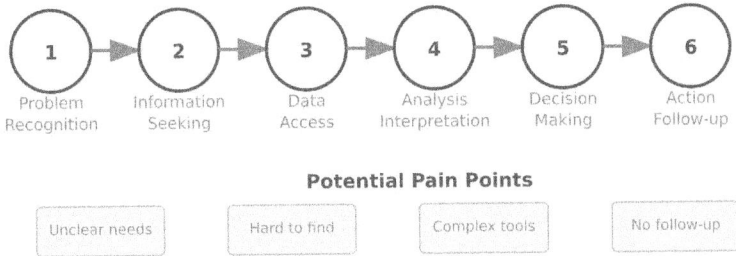

Figure 18: User Journey Map.

The journey includes problem recognition, information seeking, data access, analysis and interpretation, decision making, action, and follow-up. Each step presents opportunities for data products to add value or create friction.

User Personas for Data Products

Create detailed personas that capture not just demographics, but data-specific characteristics that shape how people interact with information and analytics.

Building Effective Personas

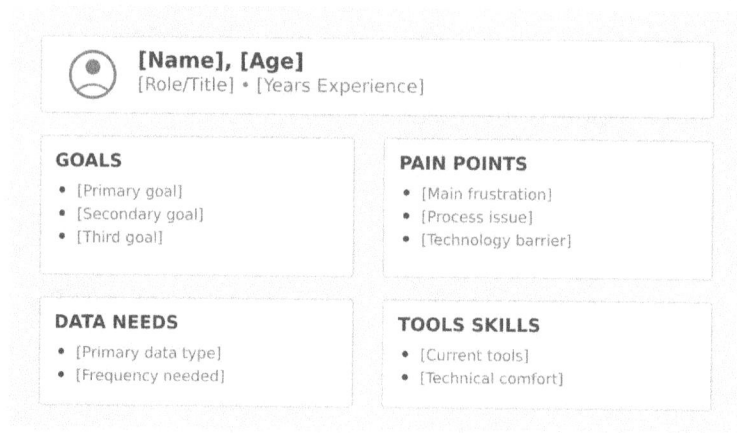

Figure 19: Persona Card Template.

Sarah, Regional Sales Manager

Sarah is 35 years old, holds an MBA, and has eight years of experience managing 12 sales representatives. Her primary goals include hitting quarterly revenue targets, developing her team's skills, and identifying new growth opportunities.

Her data needs center around weekly sales performance metrics, competitive intelligence, and pipeline health indicators. Her technical skills include comfort with Excel and CRM systems, basic SQL knowledge, and a preference for visual interfaces.

Time constraints shape how she interacts with data. She has 15-minute windows between meetings for data review and needs mobile access during client visits.

Her **decision context** includes both strategic decisions, such as quarterly planning, and tactical decisions, such as weekly coaching conversations.

Current pain points include customer data scattered across multiple systems, reports that are often out of date when she needs them, and the inability to drill down without IT help.

Her key quote captures her mindset: "I don't need perfect data, I need good enough data quickly so I can help my team succeed."

Persona Validation Process

Ensure these profiles reflect reality rather than assumptions:

1. Create initial personas based on assumptions and limited research.
2. Test with real users through interviews and observation.
3. Refine based on feedback and actual behavior data.
4. Validate with usage analytics once products are live.
5. Update regularly as roles and needs evolve.

A financial services company built sophisticated risk analytics for loan officers, but adoption was terrible: only 12% after six months.

User research revealed their persona assumptions were completely wrong. They assumed loan officers wanted detailed risk analytics, but they wanted simple red/yellow/green risk indicators. They assumed officers had time for complex analysis, but they had 3-5 minutes per application review. They assumed officers worked primarily at desks, but they actually spent 60% of their time in client meetings that required mobile access.

The redesigned product focused on simple, mobile-friendly risk indicators that could be understood at a glance. Adoption increased to 89% within three months because the product finally matched how users actually worked.

Designing for Adoption

Even well-designed data products face adoption challenges: users are comfortable with existing tools, new products require learning new interfaces, benefits aren't always immediately obvious, and fitting into existing work patterns is hard.

The HEART Framework for Data Products

I adapt Google's HEART framework for data product adoption:

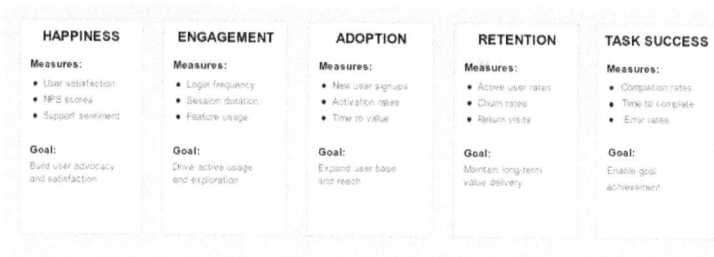

HAPPINESS	ENGAGEMENT	ADOPTION	RETENTION	TASK SUCCESS
Measures:	Measures:	Measures:	Measures:	Measures:
• User satisfaction • NPS scores • Support sentiment	• Login frequency • Session duration • Feature usage	• New user signups • Activation rates • Time to value	• Active user rates • Churn rates • Return visits	• Completion rates • Time to complete • Error rates
Goal:	Goal:	Goal:	Goal:	Goal:
Build user advocacy and satisfaction	Drive active usage and exploration	Expand user base and reach	Maintain long-term value delivery	Enable goal achievement

Figure 20: HEART Framework for Data Products.

- **Happiness** measures user satisfaction through surveys and qualitative feedback.

- **Engagement** tracks login frequency and feature usage patterns.

- **Adoption** measures new user onboarding and conversion to regular usage.

- **Retention** evaluates continued usage over time and reasons for abandonment.

- **Task Success** examines completion rates, time to achieve goals, and error rates.

Focus on the metrics that matter most for your context. Early products should emphasize adoption and task success. Mature products should optimize for engagement and retention.

The Progressive Disclosure Strategy

Don't overwhelm users with everything at once. Design for progressive sophistication that allows users to grow into complexity as their needs and skills develop.

Three Levels of Complexity

- **Level 1: Basic Consumption** provides simple, pre-built dashboards with clear visualizations and minimal customization options. Users can get value immediately without training or complex setup.

- **Level 2: Interactive Exploration** adds filtering and drill-down capabilities, simple self-service analytics, and basic customization options. Users can ask follow-up questions and explore patterns that interest them.

- **Level 3: Advanced Analytics** includes complex queries and analysis, statistical functions and modeling, advanced customization, and integration with external tools. Users can perform sophisticated analysis and create custom solutions.

Users start at Level 1 and progress as they become more comfortable and need more sophisticated capabilities. This approach prevents cognitive overload while providing growth paths for power users.

Reducing Barriers to Entry

Common Barriers and Solutions

- **Technical Barriers** include system access complexity. Solutions include single sign-on integration, mobile optimization, integration with existing tools, and minimal training requirements.

- **Cognitive Barriers** arise from interface complexity. Solutions include intuitive interfaces matching mental models, clear business language, contextual help, and progressive complexity.

- **Organizational Barriers** often prove most challenging. Solutions include management support, time allocation for learning, performance metrics rewarding data use, and proactive change management.

The Excel Integration Strategy

A manufacturing company built a production analytics platform, but plant managers continued using Excel for analysis and reporting. User research revealed the barrier: they needed to export data to Excel for regulatory compliance reports that required specific formatting. The analytics platform provided better insights, but Excel remained necessary for compliance.

We built Excel export functionality directly into the platform with pre-formatted compliance templates. This removed the last reason to avoid the new system while maintaining compliance requirements.

Adoption went from 23% to 94% in two months. Managers started using the platform for additional analysis beyond compliance because they were already there and the insights were valuable.

Building Feedback Loops and Iteration Cycles

Continuous user feedback is essential because user needs evolve, business contexts change, and product usage patterns reveal opportunities for improvement.

Multi-Channel Feedback Collection

You need multiple touchpoints that capture different types of insights:

- **In-Product Feedback** captures user sentiment at the moment of use. Quick rating systems for features provide immediate reactions. Contextual feedback forms at decision points gather input when users are most engaged. Usage analytics reveal what users actually do, rather than what they say they do.

- **Regular User Engagement** maintains ongoing relationships. Monthly user surveys track satisfaction trends. Quarterly focus groups provide deep qualitative insights. Regular office hours for direct feedback create accessible communication channels.

- **Passive Intelligence Gathering** captures insights without requiring explicit user actions. Support ticket analysis reveals common pain points. Usage pattern analysis identifies friction points where users struggle or abandon tasks. Search query analysis helps understand user intent and unmet needs.

The Monthly Iteration Cycle

- **Week 1, Collect and Analyze**: Gather feedback from the previous month, review support tickets and satisfaction scores, and analyze usage data for patterns.

- **Week 2, Plan Improvements**: Prioritize issues by business impact and user feedback, design solutions, and estimate effort.

- **Week 3, Develop and Test**: Implement fixes and improvements, test with power users, and gather feedback on proposed changes.

- **Week 4, Deploy and Communicate**: Roll out improvements to all users, communicate what changed and why, and measure initial impact.

Building User-Centric Teams

The Champion Strategy

Most teams discover they were wrong about adoption: they thought great technology would sell itself. Identify and develop champions who can drive adoption organically through peer influence.

Types of Champions

- **Power Users** love data and analytics. Give them advanced features and early access to new capabilities. Use their feedback to guide development priorities. Help them become internal advocates and trainers.

- **Influencers** are respected team members whom others follow. Ensure they have exceptional experiences with the product. Provide them with success stories and talking points. Ask them to demonstrate usage in team meetings.

- **Managers** can require or encourage usage through authority. Show them clear business value and ROI. Give them management dashboards and team performance reports. Help them create team goals around data usage.

Support these advocates through monthly champion meetings to share feedback and best practices, quarterly training sessions on new features, annual recognition and rewards, and direct communication channels with the product team.

Ethical Considerations and Trust Building

Trust forms the foundation of successful data product adoption, and transparency systematically builds that trust.

Building Trust Through Transparency

Essential Transparency Elements

- **Data Lineage** shows users where data comes from and how it's processed. When data comes from multiple systems, show the integration process. When data is transformed or calculated, explain the methodology.

- **Quality Indicators** provide an honest assessment of data limitations and confidence levels. If data is incomplete or estimated, communicate this clearly. Quality scores help users understand reliability.

- **Update Notifications** inform users about data refreshes, changes in methodology, and system updates. When calculation methods change, explain why and how it affects results.

- **Methodology Documentation** explains how metrics are calculated and what they mean. Complex calculations require simple explanations. Business definitions matter more than technical implementation details.

Privacy and Data Ethics

User Control and Consent

- **Clear Privacy Policies** explain what data is collected about users and how it's used.

- **Granular Consent** lets users control what data they share and how it's used.

- **Data Minimization** collects only the data necessary for the product to function.

- **Right to Delete** provides mechanisms for users to remove their data.

Avoiding Bias and Discrimination

- **Bias Detection** requires regularly testing for discriminatory patterns in data and algorithms.

- **Diverse Perspectives** include diverse voices in product design and testing.

- **Algorithmic Transparency** explains how automated decisions are made.

- **Human Override** provides mechanisms for users to challenge automated decisions.

Case Studies in Human-Centric Design

Case Study 1: The Sales Intelligence Transformation

A software company's sales team was scattered across multiple tools with inconsistent data and no visibility into pipeline health.

What the Research Revealed: Sales reps spent 20% of their time looking for customer information across disconnected systems. Managers needed weekly pipeline reviews but the data was always outdated. The team preferred mobile access for field work. Technical sophistication varied widely across the team.

The Design: A mobile-first interface with offline capability ensured access regardless of connectivity. Role-based dashboards provided rep views focused on individual performance and manager views emphasizing team oversight. Integration with existing CRM and communication tools reduced context switching. The product was introduced gradually, beginning with a small group of sales champions before rolling out to the wider team.

Results After 12 Months: Adoption reached 85%, up from 12% at baseline. Sales reps reduced administrative time by 30%. Forecast accuracy improved by 15%. In quarterly surveys, 92% of users rated the tool as valuable for their daily work.

Case Study 2: The Healthcare Analytics Revolution

A hospital system needed to give clinical staff better visibility into patient outcomes and operational efficiency, but previous systems had failed due to poor adoption.

What We Learned: Nurses and doctors had 30-second windows to check information between patients. Clinical staff needed alerts rather than analytics dashboards, and previous systems required too many clicks in time-pressured environments. Integration with existing electronic health records was critical.

The Design: A smart alert system integrated into existing EHR (Electronic Health Record) workflows eliminated context switching. One-click access to relevant patient analytics provided immediate information. Color-coded visual indicators required no training. Automated recommendations included a clear rationale.

Results After 18 Months: Clinical staff engagement reached 96% compared to 8% with the previous system. Patient readmission rates decreased by 22% due to better predictive insights. Patient satisfaction improved by 18%. The initiative generated $3.2M in annual savings from improved operational efficiency.

Reflection: Think about your most successful data product. What human-centered design principles contributed to its success?

Looking Forward

Understanding users is fundamental to data product success, but it's only the beginning. The next challenge is building products that can handle the complexity and speed of modern AI-driven business environments.

Key Takeaways

Users don't care about your data; they care about their problems. Starting with business problems and user needs rather than data capabilities ensures you build solutions people actually want to use.

Adoption is a product feature: design and plan for it from the beginning. Start with simple, reliable solutions that fit real workflows. You can always add sophistication later, once people are using the product.

Champions drive adoption more effectively than formal training programs or management mandates. Identify and develop advocates who can influence others and provide peer-to-peer support.

Feedback is a continuous process that should be built into product development cycles. User needs evolve, contexts change, and usage patterns reveal optimization opportunities.

Trust is earned through transparency about data sources, quality, limitations, and methodologies. Be honest about what you know and don't know. Users prefer reliable partial information to unreliable complete information.

Design for the least technical user because if it works for them, it will work for everyone. Power users can handle complexity, but broad adoption requires accessibility.

Your Next Steps

Begin by conducting user interviews for one of your current data products. Talk to 5-7 actual users about their jobs-to-be-done, current frustrations, and desired outcomes. This research often reveals gaps between assumptions and reality.

Create detailed personas for your primary user groups based on real research, not assumptions. Include data-specific characteristics such as technical comfort level, time constraints, and decision context. Map the user journey for your most important workflows to understand where users struggle and where data products can add the most value. Focus on the complete experience from problem recognition to action.

Implement a systematic feedback collection system that captures user input through multiple channels and processes it into product improvements. Establish regular user research and iteration cycles to ensure your products continue to meet user needs as they evolve. Identify and develop product champions in your organization who can drive adoption through peer influence and advocacy. Invest in these relationships because they generate more adoption than formal programs.

The most technically impressive data product in the world is worthless if humans can't or won't use it. Put users at the center of your design process, and everything else becomes easier.

SIX

AI-Ready Data Products and Quality Management

When Data Quality Becomes Mission-Critical

The data landscape has fundamentally shifted. What used to be forgiving batch processes that might delay a report are now real-time AI systems making split-second decisions that directly affect customers. Poor data quality that once meant delayed monthly reports now means immediate, visible errors that damage customer trust and trigger regulatory violations.

I'm seeing this transition firsthand: data governance teams are suddenly inheriting AI governance responsibilities because traditional AI teams often lack the foundational governance and data quality foundations required for enterprise deployment. Even in AI-enabled data products, accountability remains with the data product owner, while governance functions provide guardrails, oversight, and escalation paths.

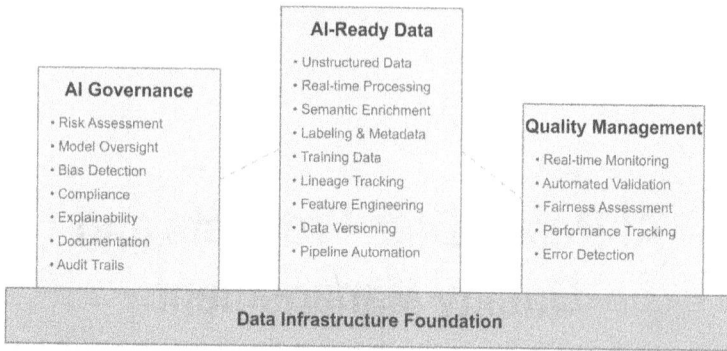

AI-Ready Data
- Unstructured Data
- Real-time Processing
- Semantic Enrichment
- Labeling & Metadata
- Training Data
- Lineage Tracking
- Feature Engineering
- Data Versioning
- Pipeline Automation

AI Governance
- Risk Assessment
- Model Oversight
- Bias Detection
- Compliance
- Explainability
- Documentation
- Audit Trails

Quality Management
- Real-time Monitoring
- Automated Validation
- Fairness Assessment
- Performance Tracking
- Error Detection

Data Infrastructure Foundation

Figure 21: AI Readiness Framework.

The stakes have escalated dramatically. The EU AI Act imposes fines up to €35 million or 7% of global turnover for serious breaches. While regulatory details vary by region, the underlying governance principles—risk classification, explainability, and accountability—are converging globally. California's AI transparency laws require explainable decision-making. Organizations can't afford to treat AI data governance and quality as an afterthought.

But there's no additional budget or headcount for this expanded scope. Data teams must evolve strategically to support AI products while maintaining excellence in traditional data operations.

Expanding Data Team Responsibilities for AI

AI systems demand new approaches that extend far beyond traditional data management. Traditional data governance asked, "Is the data clean and accessible?" AI governance asks, "Is the data clean, accessible, fair, learnable, and explainable for AI systems?" These governance extensions exist to protect and scale data products in AI contexts, not to replace product ownership or business accountability.

AI System Risk Classification

Using frameworks such as the EU AI Act, classify AI systems based on their impact and oversight requirements.

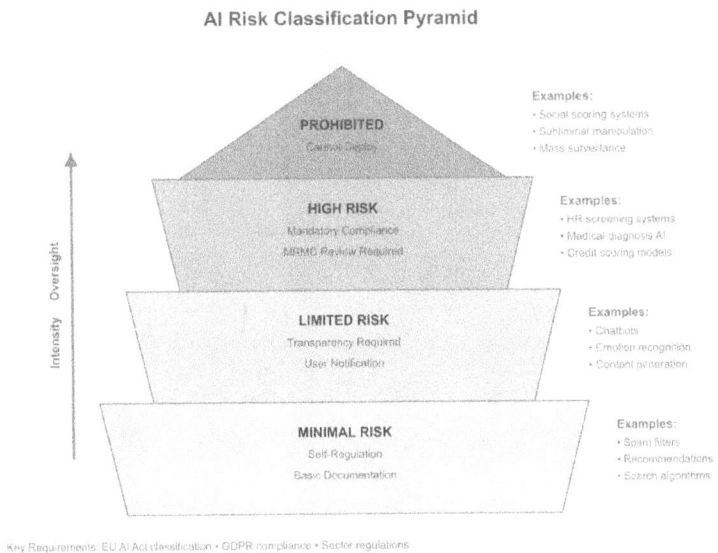

Figure 22: AI Risk Classification Pyramid.

- **Prohibited Systems,** like social scoring, cannot be deployed.

- **High Risk Systems,** such as HR screening, require mandatory compliance.

- **Limited Risk Systems,** like chatbots, need transparency obligations.

- **Minimal Risk Systems,** such as spam filters, operate under self-regulation.

This classification determines your data quality requirements, governance overhead, and compliance obligations. A simple chatbot might seem harmless until you realize it falls into a regulated category that requires explainability and bias monitoring.

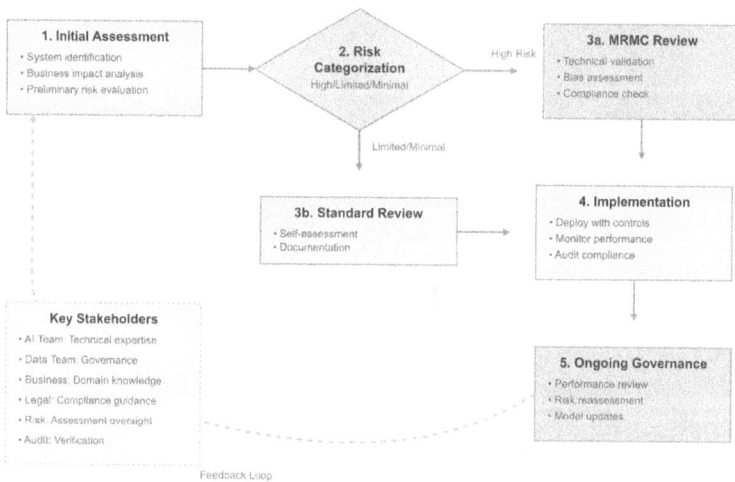

Figure 23: Model Risk Management Flow.

Create a Model Risk Management Committee (MRMC) for high-risk AI system approvals. Your AI risk assessment template should cover purpose, data sources, risk tier, key controls, and sign-off owners. Include representatives from AI, Data, Architecture, Business, Legal, and Compliance teams. Critical assessment questions help determine gaps: Is your AI team handling model behavior governance effectively? Who manages training data provenance and feedback loops? Are AI risk assessments being conducted systematically? If these capabilities are missing, they may fall into your data team's scope.

Real-World Transformation: The Legal Firm's AI Journey

A mid-sized legal firm processing 10,000 contract documents monthly decided to implement AI-powered document processing. Their traditional approach wasn't scaling: manual document review took two hours per contract.

The Problem: Their existing data governance focused on privacy and access control but lacked frameworks for AI quality and bias detection. They needed to maintain legal defensibility while dramatically improving processing speed.

The Approach: They implemented specialized legal AI models that improved OCR (Optical Character Recognition) accuracy from 87% to 98%. Processing time dropped from two hours to 15 minutes per document. Search relevance improved by 340% using semantic approaches. The solution was introduced through a controlled pilot with selected document types before expanding to broader contract categories.

The Outcome: Six months later, they were processing 15,000 documents per month with the same team size, had reduced client response times by 75%, and had improved legal review accuracy scores. Most importantly, they built AI governance capabilities that enabled expansion into other legal AI applications.

Building AI-Ready Data Products

Most data teams built their expertise around structured, batch-processed data with predictable schemas. AI systems demand something entirely different: text, audio, video, and sensor data processing with real-time requirements and semantic understanding that goes beyond format validation.

Understanding your AI initiatives' data needs helps prioritize infrastructure investments. Text data supports natural language processing and semantic search. Audio enables speech recognition and sentiment analysis. Video supports computer vision and behavior analysis. Sensor data enables predictive maintenance and anomaly detection. Documents support knowledge management and compliance.

Each type requires different processing approaches that extend well beyond traditional structured data management.

Raw data needs preprocessing pipelines tailored to each type and use case. Document processing illustrates the complexity:

- **Content extraction** uses OCR for scanned documents.

- **Structure recognition** identifies headers and tables.

- **Quality assessment** flags issues that could affect AI performance.

- **Semantic enrichment** adds context markers that help AI systems understand meaning.

In labeling and metadata management, AI systems need well-structured metadata to find and use data effectively. Good annotation improves AI precision by 40-60%. Quality depends on accuracy, consistency, and validation processes. Automation handles 80-90% of routine classifications, including document type, topic, sentiment, format standardization, and duplicate detection. But 10-20% requires human intervention for critical datasets, complex relationships, bias validation, and legal defensibility.

An another example, real-time becomes essential for customer-facing AI applications, fraud detection, personalization systems, and operational decision-making. But real-time requires different architectures, creates operational complexity, demands different scaling patterns, and makes quality assurance challenging. Not everything needs to be real-time. Save that effort for use cases where a few seconds really make or break the experience. Start with high-impact use cases, balance complexity versus benefit, and plan for graceful degradation when things fail.

Quality Management for AI Systems

In BI, a bad data point might appear in a monthly report that someone emails you. With AI, a bad data point can turn straight into a wrong decision for a real customer in real time. That changes how we think about quality. AI systems transform quality from a nice-to-have into a mission-critical requirement. In AI-enabled data products, governance is invisible to builders but transparency is essential for users: rules are automated, but behavior, confidence, and limitations must remain visible. Traditional quality approaches, checking data after processing, fixing issues reactively, and measuring quality monthly, don't work when failures affect customers immediately.

Traditional Data Quality	AI Data Quality
Primary Focus: Structural integrity and completeness "Is the data clean and formatted correctly?"	**Primary Focus:** Learning suitability and fairness "Is the data meaningful, fair, and explainable?"
Processing Model: Batch processing acceptable Delayed issue reporting tolerable	**Processing Model:** Real-time requirements essential Immediate error visibility critical
Validation Approach: Format and rule-based validation Schema compliance checking	**Validation Approach:** Semantic understanding required Context and meaning validation
Failure Impact: Delayed reports and analysis Internal process disruption	**Failure Impact:** Immediate customer-facing errors Business relationship damage
Quality Dimensions: Accuracy • Completeness • Consistency Validity • Timeliness	**Quality Dimensions:** + Fairness • Explainability • Bias Detection + Semantic Coherence • Learning Readiness

Figure 24: Data versus AI Quality Comparison.

AI quality management requires new approaches: monitor quality continuously during processing, detect and correct issues in real time before they reach users, implement fallback mechanisms when quality drops below acceptable thresholds, use confidence scores to indicate uncertainty in AI outputs, route edge cases to human review when automated systems encounter unfamiliar situations, and explain limitations clearly to users.

A comprehensive approach covers the entire AI pipeline through multiple validation layers:

- **Input Quality** validates source data and prevents problems from entering the system. Format standardization and error detection catch issues early. Completeness checking ensures AI systems have sufficient information for reliable decisions.

- **Processing Quality** addresses transformation accuracy and semantic coherence throughout the pipeline. Feature engineering validation prevents subtle errors that could affect system performance.

- **Output Quality** monitors the final results that users see and interact with. Prediction accuracy and confidence scoring help users understand reliability. Bias detection and fairness assessment prevent discriminatory outcomes. Explainability measures ensure users can understand and validate AI decisions.

- **Operational Quality** tracks overall system performance and user experience. Performance and latency monitoring ensure AI systems meet user expectations. User satisfaction tracking indicates whether quality efforts translate to business value.

Quality metrics only matter when they protect or enable business outcomes such as customer trust, regulatory exposure, revenue impact, or operational stability.

Effective monitoring requires automated systems that can keep pace with real-time operations. At a minimum, you need clear quality thresholds and alerts for when metrics drift out of bounds, routing rules that send the right issues to the right teams, and dashboards that distinguish between "noise" and genuinely critical failures. This systematic approach keeps teams focused on what really matters while catching emerging problems early.

Building AI-Ready Organizations

Understanding AI system behavior helps anticipate quality issues. Unstructured data processing becomes essential as AI systems work with diverse data types. Knowledge of bias detection and fairness assessment prevents discriminatory outcomes that could damage relationships or violate regulations. Real-time processing architectures enable immediate responses. Communication skills bridge technical complexity and business decision-making.

You don't need a brand-new AI platform, but you do need to upgrade key components to handle new workloads, especially unstructured and real-time use cases. That usually means specialized databases for semantic search, stream processing engines for real-time workloads, machine learning operations platforms for reliable deployment, and quality monitoring tools that track AI-specific metrics.

Looking Forward

AI is just the next chapter in how organizations govern, trust, and operationalize data—not a separate universe. The organizations that learn to plug AI into their existing data practices rather than treating it as magic will move faster and with more confidence than their competitors.

> AI doesn't replace traditional data product thinking—
> it extends and amplifies it.

The same principles of user focus, business value, and continuous improvement apply, but implementation requires new skills, tools, and approaches that build on established foundations.

Most organizations I work with find this transition challenging but ultimately rewarding. The capabilities you build for AI systems often improve your traditional data products as well.

Key Takeaways

AI amplifies everything, both the potential for value creation and the risks of failure. Prepare by building robust quality management systems that can handle AI's speed and complexity.

Quality becomes mission-critical because failures cause immediate business damage rather than delayed reports. Traditional approaches must evolve for real-time processing, unstructured data, and semantic understanding requirements.

AI changes how you operate: you'll need new skills, tools, and governance practices (bias detection, explainability, accountability) on top of existing foundations. Not everything needs real-time, but many AI use cases do—and data teams often end up owning more of this than they expected.

Start building unstructured data processing capabilities that can demonstrate value without risking critical operations. The future of data products is intelligent, responsive, and deeply integrated with AI systems.

Your Next Steps

Assess your AI readiness using the framework in this chapter. Identify capability gaps between the current state and AI requirements to prioritize development efforts. Determine which

AI responsibilities should belong to your data team based on organizational structure, existing skills, and strategic priorities. Consider partnering with AI teams to share governance responsibilities. Start building unstructured data processing capabilities with pilot projects. Implement quality monitoring systems designed for AI requirements, including real-time processing and bias detection.

Begin training your team on AI governance and bias detection through formal programs and hands-on experience. Establish clear partnerships with AI teams for shared responsibilities.

You don't have to fix everything this quarter. Pick one AI use case, make it safe and reliable, and build from there.

AI-readiness is not just a technical challenge; it's an operating model shift. But none of it matters if you can't take the first step. That's why the final chapter translates everything you've learned into a practical, achievable 90-day plan.

SEVEN

Your 90-Day Action Plan

The Moment of Truth

You've absorbed six chapters of frameworks, case studies, and best practices. You understand the theory of data product thinking. You can articulate the difference between data projects and data products. You know why user research matters and how to measure business value.

What will you do differently starting Monday morning?

This chapter bridges the gap between knowledge and action. It provides a concrete, practical 90-day plan to get your data product transformation started, regardless of your current organizational state or resources. The difference between organizations that successfully transform and those that don't isn't knowledge—it's execution. This plan is about execution.

The Three-Phase Approach

Based on working with dozens of organizations through this transformation, successful change happens in focused phases. Each phase builds momentum for the next while delivering tangible value along the way.

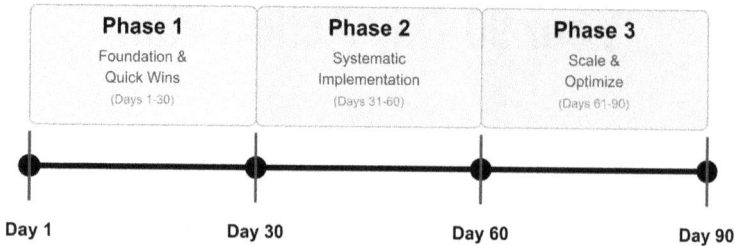

Phase 1	Phase 2	Phase 3
Foundation & Quick Wins (Days 1-30)	Systematic Implementation (Days 31-60)	Scale & Optimize (Days 61-90)

Day 1 — Day 30 — Day 60 — Day 90

Figure 25: 90-Day Timeline.

Days 1-30 establish basic product thinking and demonstrate early value. You'll build stakeholder confidence and create groundwork for sustainable change through user research and your first product launch.

Days 31-60 focus on systematic implementation. You'll roll out frameworks systematically, expand successful pilots, and begin building long-term capabilities that scale.

Days 61-90 concentrate on scaling successful approaches across multiple products while optimizing based on real-world experience. You'll also plan for continued growth beyond the initial transformation period.

Phase 1: Foundation and Quick Wins (Days 1-30)

The first 30 days are about proving that data product thinking works in your organization. You need quick, visible wins that build credibility and momentum.

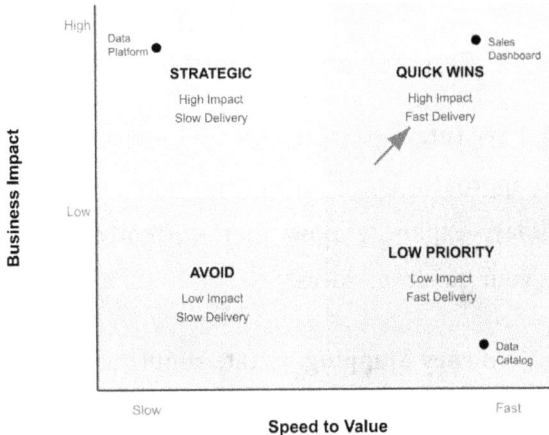

Figure 26: Quick Wins versus Long-Term Impact Matrix.

Week 1: Assessment and Planning

Day 1-2, Current State Assessment: Complete the Data Product Readiness Assessment to understand where you stand and where to focus initial efforts. Your total score indicates readiness level and priority areas for improvement.

Day 3-4, Stakeholder Mapping: Identify key stakeholders and their current data pain points. Start with executive sponsors who control the budget, primary users who would interact with data products daily, and the technical teams' current capabilities.

Day 5-7, Quick Win Identification: Building momentum requires identifying opportunities that deliver high impact with low effort. Look for existing data that could be made more accessible, manual processes that could be automated, and data quality issues affecting daily work.

Week 2: User Research and Validation

Day 8-10, User Interviews: Conduct 5-7 user interviews using a structured approach. Focus on understanding their background and workday, exploring how they currently use data, and validating your quick win ideas.

Day 11-12, Journey Mapping: Create simple user journey maps for your primary users, identifying where users get frustrated and where data products could add the most value.

Day 13-14, Solution Refinement: Refine your concepts based on research. Adjust solutions based on actual user needs, prioritize based on feedback and business impact.

Week 3: Technical Foundation

Day 15-17, Technical Assessment: Evaluate current capabilities, including available data sources, current tools and platforms, technical debt issues, and team skills and capacity.

Day 18-19, Architecture Planning: Design a simple architecture for your solutions. Keep everything simple at this stage. The goal is learning and momentum, not architectural perfection.

Day 20-21, Development Planning: Create detailed development plans by breaking work into specific tasks, identifying dependencies, and assigning responsibilities and timelines.

Week 4: Implementation and Launch

Day 22-26, Build and Test: Develop your minimum viable version and test with real data. Get feedback from two to three primary users and iterate based on their input.

Day 27-28, Soft Launch: Launch with engaged users. Provide training and support, collect detailed feedback, and monitor usage to identify issues.

Day 29-30, Evaluation and Communication: Document usage metrics and user feedback, calculate business value created, identify lessons learned, and communicate results to stakeholders.

Phase 2: Systematic Implementation (Days 31-60)

Building on your early successes, you'll now implement systematic capabilities and expand proven approaches across the organization.

Week 5-6: Framework Implementation

Day 31-35, Product Management Framework: Create detailed product charters for 2-3 additional products. Each charter should include a clear problem statement and user definition, success criteria and measurement plan, and ownership structure. Systematize your approach through regular user contact schedules, detailed personas for different user segments, and ongoing feedback collection mechanisms.

Day 36-42, Team Organization: Organize teams around products rather than technical functions. Define clear roles: assign Data Product Managers, identify Business Data Owners, establish technical ownership, and create escalation paths. Implement regular operating rhythms: weekly product team standups, bi-weekly user feedback reviews, and monthly stakeholder check-ins.

Week 7-8: Governance and Value Systems

Day 43-49, Quality and Governance Standards: Define data quality requirements in business terms, implement automated quality monitoring, establish quality issue escalation procedures, and create user-friendly quality indicators. Create simple approval processes for new products that focus on risk and value, establish data classification standards, and implement basic compliance checking.

Day 50-60, Value Measurement System: Define usage, outcome, and impact metrics for each product. Implement tracking infrastructure, create automated reporting dashboards, and establish regular review processes. Create templates for business case development and train team members on calculation methods.

Phase 3: Scale and Optimize (Days 61-90)

Scaling successful approaches across multiple products and teams while optimizing performance based on accumulated experience.

Week 9-10: Expansion and Scaling

Day 61-67, Product Portfolio Development: Shift from managing individual products to managing a portfolio. Categorize products using the Three Horizons model: products supporting current operations, extending current capabilities, and creating new capabilities. Implement value-based budgeting that allocates resources based on demonstrated and projected business value.

Day 68-74, Organizational Scaling: Expand product management skills through targeted training and coaching. Implement training programs for user research, business case development, and technical product management. Standardize successful processes while maintaining flexibility. Implement scaled governance mechanisms and create self-service tools that enable team autonomy.

Week 11-12: Optimization and Planning

Day 75-81, Performance Optimization: Analyze usage patterns and user feedback to understand actual versus intended usage. Identify performance bottlenecks and implement improvements based on data rather than assumptions. Review team structures and processes to identify improvement opportunities.

Day 82-90, Strategic Planning: Develop a comprehensive 6-month roadmap identifying the next wave of opportunities, necessary technology investments, organizational capability development, and strategic goals. Create a year one vision defining your target state for data product maturity, required investments, and scaling plans.

Implementation Accelerators

- **The Executive Sponsor Playbook:** Start with business problems, not technology solutions. Quantify current costs of poor data access and demonstrate early value creation. Connect everything to strategic objectives. Establish clear communication with monthly status updates and quarterly business reviews.

- **The Champion Network Strategy:** Identify 3-5 enthusiastic users across different departments in the first two weeks. Your champions should provide user feedback, test products, advocate for adoption, and share success stories. Support champions with monthly meetings, direct access to your team, and recognition and rewards.

- **The Change Management Toolkit**: Implement multi-channel communication through consistent messaging. Provide comprehensive training through role-specific programs, self-service resources, and regular support sessions. Manage resistance by identifying sources early, addressing concerns with evidence, and providing transition support.

Common 90-Day Pitfalls and How to Avoid Them

- **Trying to Do Too Much**: Focus on one to two high-impact opportunities maximum. Ensure your team has dedicated time for data product work.

- **Skipping User Research**: Mandate user interviews before development begins. Require user testing before launches.

- **Ignoring Organizational Change**: Invest in change management from day one. Secure executive sponsorship and visible support.

- **Perfectionism Over Progress**: Embrace "good enough" for initial launches. Focus on core user value first and plan for iteration.

Success Metrics for Your 90-Day Plan

Days 1-30: Foundation Metrics

- Number of user interviews conducted.
- Products launched and adoption rates.
- Number of active sponsors and champions.
- Training completed and skills developed.

Days 31-60: Implementation Metrics

- Number of products under active management.
- Quantified business value delivered.
- Governance processes implemented.
- Net Promoter Score from business users.

Days 61-90: Scale Metrics

- Departments and user groups served.
- ROI and cost savings achieved.
- Team members trained and certified.
- Connection to business objectives.

Overall Success Indicators: By day 90, aim for at least $500K in quantified annual value, 75%+ adoption rate for launched products, 8.0+ satisfaction scores from key stakeholders, and a team that feels confident about scaling to the next phase.

Your Day 91 Planning Session

Conduct a comprehensive planning session for the next phase:

- **Results Review**: Quantify business value created, document lessons learned, identify most successful approaches, and celebrate wins while recognizing contributors.

- **Capability Assessment**: Evaluate current organizational capabilities, identify gaps, plan for continued development, and design scaling strategies.

- **Strategic Planning**: Connect data products to business strategy, identify next opportunities, plan for platform investments, and set ambitious 12-month goals.

Final Thoughts: From Plan to Transformation

Your 90-day plan is designed to put users at the center from day one. This plan creates momentum, demonstrates value, and builds the foundation for lasting change. But transformation doesn't happen in 90 days. It happens because of what you do in the first 90 days. Organizations that successfully transform share common characteristics: they start with users, not technology; focus on business value, not technical elegance; build momentum through early wins; invest in people and capabilities; and embrace experimentation and learning.

Your 90-day plan is not a destination—it's the beginning of a journey toward becoming a truly data-driven organization. Use this plan as a starting point, but adapt it to your specific context, challenges, and opportunities.

The most important step is the first one. The second most important step is the one after that. Just keep moving.

Your Immediate Next Steps

- **Tomorrow**: Complete the readiness assessment and stakeholder mapping.

- **This Week**: Conduct your first three user interviews.

- **Next Week**: Identify and commit to your first quick win.

- **This Month**: Launch your first data product and measure results.

Begin with a small, manageable step and expand over time. The question isn't whether it will transform your industry—it's whether you'll help lead that transformation.

Years ago, I saw a Ferrari no one drove. Today, I see organizations learning to hand the keys to everyone, building data products people actually use.

Organizations that embrace this approach early will gain an advantage.

About the Author

Amy Raygada is a Principal Data and AI Strategist at Thoughtworks and Founder of CosmoData Management. Over almost two decades, she's helped global organizations transform their data and AI capabilities, specializing in the crucial bridge between business strategy and technical implementation.

Her work spans industries from retail and automotive to financial services and media, guiding leaders through the messy reality of turning data strategy into business results. She's learned that the most elegant technical architectures mean nothing if people can't or won't use them—a lesson that appears throughout every chapter of this book.

Amy is a recognized voice in the data community, serving as a keynote speaker and panelist at international conferences including Big Data London, Data Masterclass Europe, and Women in Data and AI. She's also the creator of the Data Chronicles live show and author of the course "Data and AI Product Management: Learn to discover, strategize, and show value in the age of AI" for O'Reilly Media.

Her passion lies in making data strategy practical, human-centered, and sustainable. She's spent years watching organizations struggle with the gap between technical possibility and business adoption, which led to the frameworks and approaches you've read in these pages.

References and Bibliography

Case Study Sources and Methodology

Note: Specific company names and details have been anonymized throughout this book to protect client confidentiality. Case studies represent composite examples based on multiple real-world implementations across the following sectors:

- **Financial Services:** Banking, insurance, and investment management organizations.

- **Healthcare and Life Sciences:** Hospitals, pharmaceutical companies, and healthcare technology providers.

- **Retail and E-commerce:** Traditional retailers and digital-native commerce companies.

- **Manufacturing and Supply Chain:** Industrial manufacturers and logistics providers.

- **Technology:** Software companies and technology service providers.

All quantified results and success metrics are based on actual client engagements conducted between 2020 and 2024, with data aggregated and anonymized to protect organizational confidentiality while maintaining practical relevance.

Core Methodologies and Frameworks

Baghai, Mehrdad, Stephen Coley, and David White. The Alchemy of Growth: Practical Insights for Building the Enduring Enterprise. Perseus Publishing, 1999. Source of Three Horizons model adapted for data product portfolio management

Christensen, Clayton M., Taddy Hall, Karen Dillon, and David S. Duncan. Competing Against Luck: The Story of Innovation and Customer Choice. Harvard Business Review Press, 2016. Foundation for Jobs-To-Be-Done framework applied to data products

Dehghani, Zhamak. Data Mesh: Delivering Data-Driven Value at Scale. O'Reilly Media, 2022. Comprehensive guide to data mesh architecture and organizational patterns

User Experience and Product Management

Rodden, Kerry, Hilary Hutchinson, and Xin Fu. "Measuring User Happiness." Proceedings of the SIGCHI Conference on Human Factors in Computing Systems, 2010, pp. 2063-2066. HEART framework for measuring user-centered product success

Torres, Teresa. Continuous Discovery Habits: Discover Products that Create Customer Value and Business Value. Product Talk LLC, 2021. Modern product discovery techniques applied to data product development

Data Quality and Governance

DAMA International. DAMA-DMBOK: Data Management Body of Knowledge, 2nd Edition. Technics Publications, 2017. Comprehensive reference for data management principles and practices

Redman, Thomas C. Getting in Front on Data: Who Does What. Technics Publications, 2016. Foundational principles for data quality management and organizational accountability

AI Governance and Regulatory Compliance

European Commission. "Regulation (EU) 2024/1689 on Artificial Intelligence (EU AI Act)." Official Journal of the European Union, 2024. Legal framework for AI system classification and compliance requirements

National Institute of Standards and Technology. AI Risk Management Framework (AI RMF 1.0). NIST, 2023. Practical framework for managing AI risks in enterprise environments

Value Measurement and Business Impact

Davenport, Thomas H., and D.J. Patil. "Data Scientist: The Sexiest Job of the 21st Century." *Harvard Business Review*, vol. 90, no. 10, 2012, pp. 70-76. *Early articulation of data professional roles and business value creation*

Organizational Design and Change Management

Kotter, John P. *Leading Change.* Harvard Business Review Press, 1996. *Change management principles applied to data transformation initiatives*

Skelton, Matthew, and Manuel Pais. Team Topologies: Organizing Business and Technology Teams for Fast Flow. IT Revolution Press, 2019. Team organization patterns adapted for data product organizations

Technology and Architecture

Kleppmann, Martin. Designing Data-Intensive Applications. O'Reilly Media, 2017. Technical foundations for scalable data systems and quality management

Newman, Sam. Building Microservices: Designing Fine-Grained Systems, 2nd Edition. O'Reilly Media, 2021. Microservices architecture principles applied to data platforms

Standards and Compliance Frameworks

California Consumer Privacy Act (CCPA). California Civil Code Section 1798.100-1798.199, 2018. *State-level privacy regulations for data handling and user rights*

General Data Protection Regulation (GDPR). "Regulation (EU) 2016/679." Official Journal of the European Union, 2016. Privacy regulations affecting data product design and governance

ISO/IEC 25012:2008. "Software Engineering — Software Product Quality Requirements and Evaluation (SQuaRE) — Data Quality Model." International standards for data quality measurement and evaluation

Professional Development and Training

International Association for Privacy Professionals (IAPP). "Privacy Engineering Resources." https://iapp.org/ *Privacy by design principles for data product development*

Index

www.ingramcontent.com/pod-product-compliance
Lightning Source LLC
Chambersburg PA
CBHW071423210326
41597CB00020B/3632